State and Local Intelligence
in the War
on Terrorism

K. Jack Riley

Gregory F. Treverton

Jeremy M. Wilson

Lois M. Davis

T0159318

RAND INFRASTRUCTURE, SAFETY,
AND ENVIRONMENT

The research described in this report results from the RAND Corporation's continuing program of self-initiated research. Support for such research is provided, in part, by donors and by the independent research development provisions of RAND's contracts for the operation of its U.S. Department of Defense federally funded research and development centers. This research was conducted within RAND Infrastructure, Safety, and Environment (ISE), a unit of the RAND Corporation.

Library of Congress Cataloging-in-Publication Data

State and local intelligence in the war on terrorism / K. Jack Riley... [et al.].
    p. cm.
    "MG-394."
    Includes bibliographical references.
    ISBN 0-8330-3859-1 (pbk. : alk. paper)
    1. War on Terrorism, 2001– 2. Law enforcement. 3. Intelligence service.
    4. Terrorism—Prevention. I. Riley, Kevin Jack, 1964–

    HV6432.7.S737 2005
    363.32'0973—dc22

2005027743

The RAND Corporation is a nonprofit research organization providing objective analysis and effective solutions that address the challenges facing the public and private sectors around the world. RAND's publications do not necessarily reflect the opinions of its research clients and sponsors.

RAND® is a registered trademark.

Cover design by Stephen Bloodsworth

Published 2005 by the RAND Corporation
1776 Main Street, P.O. Box 2138, Santa Monica, CA 90407-2138
1200 South Hayes Street, Arlington, VA 22202-5050
201 North Craig Street, Suite 202, Pittsburgh, PA 15213-1516
RAND URL: http://www.rand.org/
To order RAND documents or to obtain additional information, contact
Distribution Services: Telephone: (310) 451-7002;
Fax: (310) 451-6915; Email: order@rand.org

Preface

Terrorism respects no boundaries. It is both a foreign and domestic matter, one that requires responses from both intelligence and law enforcement agencies, among many other entities. One aspect of combating terrorism that is often discussed but seldom examined in detail is the overlap of intelligence and law enforcement and the role of state and local law enforcement agencies as the ultimate "eyes and ears" in the war on terrorism. This report helps fill that gap by examining how state and local law enforcement agencies conducted and supported counterterrorism intelligence activities after 9/11. The research results from the RAND Corporation's continuing program of self-initiated research. Support for such research is provided, in part, by donors and by the independent research and development provisions of RAND's contracts for the operation of its U.S. Department of Defense federally funded research and development centers.

This report is one of several produced by RAND in recent years that address issues of domestic intelligence and law enforcement. Readers interested in these topics may also wish to obtain copies of the following RAND reports:

- *Collecting the Dots: Problem Formulation and Solution Elements*, Martin C. Libicki and Shari Lawrence Pfleeger, OP-103-RC, 2004.
- *Confronting "The Enemy Within": Security Intelligence, the Police, and Counterterrorism in Four Democracies*, Peter Chalk and William Rosenau, MG-100-RC, 2004.

- *Out of the Ordinary: Finding Hidden Threats by Analyzing Un-usual Behavior*, John S. Hollywood, Diane Snyder, Kenneth McKay, and John E. Boon, MG-126-RC, 2004.
- *Training the 21st Century Police Officer: Redefining Police Profes-sionalism for the Los Angeles Police Department*, Russell W. Glenn, Barbara R. Panitch, Dionne Barnes-Proby, Elizabeth F. Williams, John Christian, Matthew W. Lewis, Scott Gerwehr, and David Brannan, MR-1745-LAPD, 2003.
- *When Terrorism Hits Home: How Prepared Are State and Local Law Enforcement?* Lois M. Davis, K. Jack Riley, Gregory Kirk Ridgeway, Jennifer E. Pace, Sarah K. Cotton, Paul S. Steinberg, Kelly Damphousse, and Brent L. Smith, MG-104-MIPT, 2004.

Questions or comments on this report are welcome and can be addressed to the authors, Greg_Treverton@rand.org, Jack_Riley@rand.org, Jeremy_Wilson@rand.org, or Lois_Davis@rand.org.

This research was conducted within RAND Infrastructure, Safety, and Environment (ISE), a unit of the RAND Corporation. The mission of ISE is to improve the development, operation, use, and protection of society's essential man-made and natural assets; and to enhance the related social assets of safety and security of individuals in transit and in their workplaces and communities. The ISE research portfolio encompasses research and analysis on a broad range of policy areas including homeland security, criminal justice, public safety, occupational safety, the environment, energy, natural resources, climate, agriculture, economic development, transportation, information and telecommunications technologies, space exploration, and other aspects of science and technology policy.

Inquiries regarding RAND Infrastructure, Safety, and Environment may be directed to:

Debra Knopman, Vice President and Director
RAND ISE
1200 South Hayes Street,
Arlington, VA 22202
703-413-1100

Contents

Tables

Summary

Most discussion of information sharing in the war on terrorism has concentrated on the federal government.[1] Yet, state and local law enforcement agencies (LEAs) may be uniquely positioned to augment federal intelligence capabilities by virtue of their presence in nearly every American community, their knowledge of local individuals and groups, and their use of intelligence to combat crime. How widespread is counterterrorism intelligence activity among state and local LEAs, and how is this activity managed? What are those state and local authorities doing differently since 9/11 in collecting and processing information? How are courts and other oversight bodies guiding that process? And what might an "ideal" division of labor among the various levels of government look like?

As a starting point, this report asks how state and local intelligence activities have developed in the post–9/11 environment. We focus on LEAs' involvement in intelligence activities designed to counter terrorist actions and support national security objectives. These activities may range from investigation of possible criminal acts that are predicates of terrorist activity, including by means of electronic surveillance (typically, surveillance activities authorized by Ti-

---

[1] Joint Task Force on Intelligence and Law Enforcement (1995) is notable for its comprehensive treatment of the intersection of law enforcement and intelligence at all stages. Other examples that address domestic and foreign intelligence issues include National Commission on Terrorism (2000); Advisory Panel to Assess Domestic Response Capabilities for Terrorism Involving Weapons of Mass Destruction ("Gilmore Commission"), 1999–2004; and National Commission on Terrorist Attacks Upon the United States (2004). See also Shelby (2002).

tle III) to data collection that is incident to the normal activities of LEA officers but that is divorced from any specific criminal case (typically handed "over the wall"[2] to the FBI for its continued pursuit and intelligence-building). These activities may occur collaboratively with other agencies. We also examine state and local LEA intelligence activity that might occur under federal supervision, such as through participation on a Federal Bureau of Investigation (FBI) joint terrorism task force (JTTF). Although we describe many non-intelligence measures, perceptions, and activities in this report, we provide such reporting primarily for context.

We assess these developments in three major parts. First, we analyze data from a 2002 survey of law enforcement preparedness. Although major elements of that survey were analyzed in another report (Davis et al., 2004), this report examines survey components that were previously not analyzed or were not analyzed in the context of intelligence. This portion of the report helps us determine the breadth, scale, and dimensionality of post–9/11 LEA counter-terrorism intelligence activities.

Second, we conducted case studies of individual law enforcement agencies and their post–9/11 intelligence activities. Drawing on themes that emerged from the survey analysis, we

- assess in detail how eight LEAs around the country formed, managed, and oversaw their intelligence activities
- describe the structure, tasking, and costs associated with their intelligence operations
- review personnel and training issues associated with their programs

---

[2] The "wall" refers to perceived and actual limits on the ability to share information across criminal and intelligence investigations. Since the FBI conducts both criminal and intelligence investigations, much of the concern about the wall focuses on the FBI. Our reference to handing a matter "over the wall" refers to the general problem of managing the interface between criminal and intelligence matters. For more on the wall, see Martin (2004) and National Commission on Terrorist Attacks Upon the United States (2004).

- discuss the information sources they use in their intelligence activities, and analyze communication within and among
  agencies.

This portion of the report provides depth to our understanding of
how LEAs operate and manage their intelligence functions.

Third, we analyzed available statistics on wiretaps and related
oversight activities to gain perspective on how state and local LEA
intelligence programs combine to contribute to national intelligence
activities. This section also gives perspective on the federal role in
shaping and defining state and local LEA intelligence activity and
helps identify points of potential influence.

We conclude with a discussion of the policy implications of state
and local involvement in counterterrorism intelligence. What are the
outstanding issues and what issues might emerge in the future?

Survey Results

RAND fielded a survey in late 2002 that examined domestic preparedness, particularly among law enforcement agencies, for acts of terrorism. That work was published in 2004 as *When Terrorism Hits
Home: How Prepared Are State and Local Law Enforcement?* (Davis et
al., 2004). The 2002 survey built on previous RAND work conducted in 1994 in the aftermath of the first attack on the World
Trade Center in 1993 (Riley and Hoffman, 1995). Both reports
found high degrees of local variation in preparedness for terrorism
and a correlation between agency size and likelihood of increased
preparedness. Neither report examined intelligence issues in any detail.

For this report, we analyzed data from the 2002 survey through
the prism of intelligence. We examined LEAs' prior experience with
and perceptions of terrorism, the formation of specialized counterterrorism and intelligence units, LEAs' coordination of counterterrorism
and intelligence activities, their information sharing practices, their
terrorism threat assessment activities, and the counterterrorism and

intelligence support needs that they identified. The survey was administered to a stratified, random sample of 209 local LEAs and all 50 state-level LEAs. There are nearly 18,000 LEAs across the United States, of which approximately 1,000 have 100 or more full-time sworn officers (BJS, 2002).

State agencies generally report greater awareness of group operations and threats than local agencies do. Likewise, state entities have greater experience with incident management and response, incident investigations, and hoaxes. About 16 percent of local LEAs have specialized terrorism units, whereas 75 percent of states report having such units. Local LEA terror units typically have a more proscribed mission (primarily information-sharing); state LEA terror units are more likely to take on more expansive roles, such as training.

Most state and local LEAs have conducted terrorism threat assessments. Local LEAs were more likely to have conducted theirs after 9/11; about half of the states had done theirs prior to 9/11. There is a correlation between the size of LEAs and their threat assessment activity: the larger the local LEA, the more likely it is to have done a threat assessment.

About one-third of local LEAs collaborate with the FBI's JTTFs. The larger the local LEA, the more likely it will have participated in a JTTF. The local participation in JTTFs typically revolves around information sharing and receipt of training. Nearly all state LEAs collaborate with JTTFs for the same reasons—as well as for more expansive reasons, such as to assist with investigations. Most state LEAs and a near majority of local LEAs report needing more and better threat information. Most state LEAs and one-third of local LEAs report needing more manpower.

Generally, we can expect that the situation has changed, and perhaps improved dramatically, since the survey was fielded in late 2002. The field of intelligence is dynamic and fast-moving, and a survey conducted in 2002 cannot provide insight into the contemporary dimensions of the issue. The survey, however, did give us an idea of what types of issues to address through the cases studies. In addition, the survey points to the need to develop a mechanism that authorities could use to periodically assess the state of affairs with respect to federal, state, and local cooperation on intelligence issues. There are multiple ways that such a scorecard could be prepared, such as through the administration of an annual or biannual survey, and multiple potential institutional hosts for the scorecard, including the FBI and the Director, National Intelligence. Regardless of the method and the institutional host, however, it seems prudent to begin to track progress on the issue more systematically. The 2002 survey should be considered a baseline against which future progress can be measured.

Case Studies

The case study section analysis was organized around six thematic areas, each of which parallels a topic addressed in the survey:

- intelligence mandate and guidelines
- oversight
- counterterrorism structure, tasks, and costs
- personnel and training
- information sources
- communication within and among agencies.

Detailed interviews with local LEAs confirmed the survey finding that local police departments generally have not created separate units for the counterterrorism intelligence function. Counterterrorism intelligence gathering and analysis tend to occur as part of a larger criminal intelligence unit. Nor has the terrorist threat led to large-scale changes in the organizational structure of most local police departments.

In general, the mandate of the counterterrorism function is informal and set by the chain of command. Local police departments rely on federal guidelines in shaping their intelligence function, but the terrorist threat has raised awareness about what should and can be done in intelligence gathering, analysis, retention, and dissemination.

In turn, some departments have adopted or refined their own guidelines.

Similarly, oversight of counterterrorism intelligence is provided internally through the chain of command in most agencies. Some jurisdictions have a degree of oversight by an external body—a civilian committee, for instance, approves the Los Angeles Police Department's undercover operations.

Local police have increased their commitment of human resources to counterterrorism efforts, usually at the expense of other policing areas. Most local departments have little capacity to analyze the information they collect or receive; although federal grants have been available, most of that money has been used for equipment and consequence management, not analysis and training. The 9/11 attacks led to a sharp increase in the amount of counterterrorism information that is shared within and among local police and their federal counterparts. Paradoxically, however, the sheer number of cooperating agencies sometimes inhibits progress in responding to the terrorist threat.

Oversight and Links to National Intelligence Activity

Overall, state and local intelligence gathering has increased, at least as measured by wiretaps by law enforcement for national security intelligence purposes. Not surprisingly, the jump was sharpest from 2000 to 2001. Since 2001, the number of orders has stayed roughly constant, but the number of communications intercepted under each order has gone up sharply, nearly tripling from 2000 to 2003. The interviews—with the Las Vegas Metropolitan Police Department, for instance—confirmed that if the local LEAs undertook terrorism-related surveillance for intelligence purposes (as opposed to law enforcement), they almost always did so with federal officials through the JTTFs and with federal court oversight.

This is probably close to the ideal division of labor. Federal authorities—the FBI in particular—will naturally lead in intelligence gathering that is not connected to criminal investigation. Local LEAs have neither money nor capacity for that kind of pure intelligence. So their intelligence gathering would be guided by federal regulations and overseen primarily by federal courts.

Considerable attention has been paid to information sharing, especially from the federal level down—for instance by the national 9/11 Commission (National Commission on Terrorist Attacks Upon the United States, 2004). Although technology remains a problem, policy is a more formidable obstacle. As both the surveys and case studies suggest, the principal information-sharing mechanism, the JTTF, is constrained because state and local participants are required to have security clearances at the level of their FBI counterparts. It is imperative to find new ways to share information and to share it more widely.

Finally, while an ideal division of labor would have more analysis done at the federal than at the local level, the paucity of local capacity was striking. Only the very largest police departments have any capacity at all. The importance of analysis derives directly from the nature of the counterterrorism task. A traditional law enforcement investigation seeks to reconstruct the single trail from crime back to perpetrator. In contrast, the counterterrorism investigation, especially one aimed at prevention, must look at a number of paths— assembling enough information about each to know when patterns are changing or something suspicious is afoot along one of them. The local role in the analytic labor would be to take the general guidance provided by federal authorities and relate it to local domain awareness.

Policy Implications

The survey revealed the extent to which LEAs are engaging in counterterrorism intelligence activity. The bulk of this activity is concentrated among larger departments. The case studies provided insight into how LEAs organize and support their counterterrorism activities. Here we found that departments are not generally engaged in massive reorganizations, but rather are typically paying for these activities "out of their own hides." That is, they typically are not receiving explicit federal support and are paying for the activity out of internal reallocations. Finally, the section on authorization and oversight revealed that there has been a substantial increase in state and local involvement in wiretap activity and that the federal courts almost always retain oversight authority.

In short, the picture of law enforcement involvement in counterterrorism intelligence is somewhat mixed. On the one hand, it is probably not as pervasive as feared among civil libertarians, in the sense that relatively few LEAs appear to be supporting such activities to any great extent. On the other hand, there has been a marked increase in intelligence activity among those departments that are engaged in it.

Against this backdrop, the report considers four major issues that need to be addressed:

- *The sustainability of state and local LEA intelligence activity is in question.* State and local LEAs report that the funding for these activities is not coming from the federal government but is being borne by their budgets. It remains unclear whether LEAs will continue to support this activity as other demands on them increase. In addition, it is unclear whether intelligence activities assist with or detract from traditional crime prevention activities at the local level. This is an important issue that deserves analytic attention.
- *The training of LEA personnel involved in intelligence activity appears insufficient.* There is obvious need for more training, especially in analysis, at the state and local level. Current efforts are ad hoc and vary widely among the states. Organizations too must be "trained" to develop clear mission statements, adopt minimum standards for data collection, develop proper file maintenance standards, and implement appropriate staff training and certification processes.
- *Scant doctrine for shaping state and local LEA intelligence activity exists.* More vigorous use of the JTTFs as a locus for shaping LEA intelligence activities is one possible way of providing the

fundamental principles. Another option is the development of a federal intelligence support program that would be similar in structure and role to the position of federal security director at airports—institutions that are typically locally managed. That is, the support director would provide day-to-day operational intelligence direction. An intermediate option would be to link provision of federal funding to specific standards and practices. This list is not exhaustive, and we make no recommendation about which option might be best. Rather, we simply point out the potential for doctrinal guidance of what is a fairly loose and ad hoc process at this point.

• *The courts—the federal courts in particular—will continue to strike the balance between privacy and civil liberties, on the one hand, and national security on the other.* What our survey and case studies hinted at became much more explicit when we talked with federal homeland security intelligence officials. They feel they have little guidance when deciding what they should do with information they collect—especially about American citizens. Can they keep it in databases? For how long and on what basis? It will be up to the courts to enforce guidelines when constitutional or statutory standards apply and to put pressure on the executive branch to issue clear guidelines when such standards do not apply.

Acknowledgments

We are grateful to those who took the time to respond to RAND's earlier surveys and, especially, to those from the local police departments who agreed to be interviewed, in some detail, for the case study portion of the report. In addition to those we do not name, we offer specific thanks to Sergeant Johnny Jennings of the Charlotte-Mecklenberg Police Department, Deputy Chief John Rockwell of the Columbus Division of Police, Lieutenant Roger Kelly (Coordinator for the National Capital Regional Intelligence Center) of the Fairfax County Police Department, Deputy Chief Mike McClary and Captain Kathy Suey of the Las Vegas Metropolitan Police Department, Captain Gary Williams of the Los Angeles Police Department, Lieutenant Chris Ball of the San Diego Police Department, and Assistant Chief Alfred Broadbent of the Washington, D.C., Metropolitan Police Department.

We are also grateful to our reviewers: Cliff Karchmer of the Police Executive Research Forum; Elizabeth Rindskopf-Parker of the McGeorge School of Law, University of the Pacific; and David Brannan and John MacDonald of RAND. Cliff has been at the forefront of the debate about law enforcement intelligence; Elizabeth is an influential voice in intelligence and national security debates; David is an expert on counterterrorism issues; and John is a keen observer of law enforcement and organizational issues. All four are very knowledgeable about police institutions, and they contributed substantially to the improvement of this report. As always, Miriam Polon's red editing pen has improved the quality of our work.

To these good people we repeat our gratitude, while holding all of them blameless for any gremlins that may remain.

Acronyms

ATTF	anti-terrorism task force
CDP	Columbus (Ohio) Division of Police
CFR	Code of Federal Regulations
CMPD	Charlotte-Mecklenberg (N.C.) Police Department
COPS	Community Oriented Policing Services
DHS	Department of Homeland Security
DOJ	Department of Justice
ECPA	Electronic Communications Privacy Act
FBI	Federal Bureau of Investigation
FCPD	Fairfax County (Va.) Police Department
FISA	Foreign Intelligence Surveillance Act
INS	Immigration and Naturalization Service
JTTF	joint terrorism task force
LAPD	Los Angeles Police Department
LEA	law enforcement agency
LEIU	Law Enforcement Intelligence Unit
LVMPD	Las Vegas Metropolitan Police Department
ODP	Office of Domestic Preparedness, U.S. Department of Homeland Security
OPD	Oakland Police Department

SDPD	San Diego Police Department
S&P	standards and procedures
WDCMPD	Washington, D.C., Metropolitan Police Department

CHAPTER ONE

Introduction

What Is Intelligence?

State and local law enforcement agencies (LEAs) are valuable intelligence assets. They are the "eyes and ears" in the war on terrorism. For example, through their routine involvement in preventing and responding to crime, LEAs are believed to be well-positioned to develop information on crimes, activities, and organizations that support terrorist operations. Yet most attention remains focused on the federal level, and—good intentions notwithstanding—sharing intelligence and information among the levels of authority that make up the intelligence system remains haphazard.[1] As a recent Markle Foundation task force put it: "DHS [the Department of Homeland Security] has yet to articulate a vision of how it will link federal, state, and local agencies in a communications and sharing network, or what its role will be with respect to the TTIC [the federal Terrorist Threat

---

[1] Joint Task Force on Intelligence and Law Enforcement (1995) is notable for its comprehensive treatment of the intersection of law enforcement and intelligence at all stages. Other examples that address domestic and foreign intelligence issues include National Commission on Terrorism (2000); Advisory Panel to Assess Domestic Response Capabilities for Terrorism Involving Weapons of Mass Destruction ("Gilmore Commission"), 1999–2004; and National Commission on Terrorist Attacks Upon the United States (2004). See also Shelby (2002).

Integration Center] and other federal agencies" (Markle Foundation, 2003, p. 8).[2]

Intelligence can be defined many ways. In its most traditional form, it means information that is gathered clandestinely through eavesdropping or other data collection methods. Intelligence is typically not acted on immediately. Rather, it is usually gathered to provide a longer-term view of a problem and shape longer-term interventions. In contrast, *evidence* may be gathered through similar methods, but it is used to support the prosecution of a criminal case. Finally, *information* is gathered through open sources and collated in much the same way as intelligence to provide a more strategic view of a problem. The distinction is that information gathering does not involve using electronic surveillance and other methods of traditional intelligence gathering.

With respect to terrorist acts committed in the United States, the Federal Bureau of Investigation (FBI) is the only organization that engages in all three types of counterterrorism intelligence—information gathering, evidence gathering, and traditional intelligence. Prior to 9/11, the FBI focused on the first two activities. The extent to which it engaged in traditional intelligence was largely confined to efforts to counter the Soviet and other foreign spy threat.

State and local law enforcement agencies primarily engage in information and evidence gathering. These activities are potentially significant for counterterrorism intelligence in a number of respects. First, information and evidence gathering may help shape future traditional intelligence efforts (and may also help reduce the spending of traditional intelligence resources on unnecessary targets). In addition, evidence gathering can support traditional intelligence activities under certain circumstances.[3] Finally, and significantly, state and local

---

[2] For some of the structural and operational challenges facing intelligence agencies, see Treverton (2003). For a prescient account of intelligence challenges written prior to 9/11, see Berkowitz and Goodman (2000). The TTIC has since been replaced by the National Counterterrorism Center.

[3] For an overview of how state and local efforts may support federal efforts, see Mueller (2005).

evidence gathering may result in prosecutions that disrupt or prevent planned terrorist activities.

State and local agencies also provide direct support to traditional intelligence activities, primarily through participation in FBI joint terrorism task forces (JTTFs). In a JTTF, intelligence, homeland security, and law enforcement authorities from federal, state, and local agencies collaborate on terrorism prevention and intelligence under the supervision of the FBI. State and local authorities may contribute specialized skills (such as language capabilities or the ability to better penetrate specific groups). State and local authorities almost always subsidize the federal operations by paying for the costs of their task force participation. Approximately 100 JTTFs are currently in operation, a substantial increase over the handful that operated prior to 9/11.

For purposes of this report, we are interested in all three types of activities to the extent they support *counterterrorism efforts*. That is, we are interested in information and evidence gathering that state and local agencies undertake in support of counterterrorism efforts, but not such activities as they relate to other issues, such as organized crime, drugs, and so forth. We refer to state and local LEA involvement in all three types of intelligence activity as *counterterrorism intelligence* to distinguish it from other state and local LEA intelligence, information, and evidence gathering activities.

One key way—but not the only way—of building intelligence is through wiretaps. Although wiretaps are generally illegal in the United States, the federal government and many states have been authorized through federal and state legislation to intercept wire and electronic communications under the power of a court order. The basic wiretap power stems from two pieces of federal legislation: Title III of the Omnibus Crime Control and Safe Streets Act of 1968 and the Foreign Intelligence Surveillance Act (FISA) of 1978. Title III generally governs criminal investigations; FISA governs intelligence and counterintelligence operations and is a tool reserved exclusively for federal use. Federal and state statutes have been modified to keep pace with technologies such as mobile phones, caller ID, and modem and computer communications. The USA Patriot Act expanded Title

III (criminal) authorities to include offenses such as use of chemical weapons, bombings, computer fraud and abuse, and terrorism.[4] Generally, Title III intercepts support the building of criminal cases, whereas FISA intercepts support the conduct of intelligence activities. A frequent source of contention is whether it is appropriate to share information obtained (pass it "over the wall") under a criminal probe (from a Title III intercept) with intelligence authorities. The Patriot Act clarifies and expands on the circumstances under which foreign intelligence material obtained from a Title III intercept can be shared with intelligence agencies.

Organization of the Report

As a starting point for thinking about the roles of state and local law enforcement agencies and how they might work with federal authorities, we ask how state and local authorities have reshaped their organizations and activities in light of the terrorist threat. In particular, what capacities have they developed to collect and analyze information or intelligence, especially information not predicated on probable cause that a crime has been committed? And how have the courts and other oversight bodies responded? What guidelines, processes, or significant cases have resulted? We address these issues in Chapters Two through Four.

Chapter Two outlines the results of a nationwide survey of state and local law enforcement agencies that RAND conducted in fall 2002, one year following the 9/11 terrorist attacks, to examine their preparedness activities for terrorism.[5] The chapter analyzes the 2002 survey through the prism of intelligence.

---

[4] For an overview of the relationship of the USA Patriot Act to Title III issues, see Mueller (2005).

[5] The National Memorial Institute for the Prevention of Terrorism in Oklahoma City funded the survey; its main results are reported in other RAND reports. A more detailed analysis of the survey can be found in Davis et al. (2004).

Chapter Three turns from the survey results to look at specific cases—the Charlotte-Mecklenburg (N.C.) Police Department, the Columbus (Ohio) Division of Police, the Fairfax County (Va.) Police Department, the Las Vegas Metropolitan Police Department, the Los Angeles Police Department, the Oakland Police Department, the San Diego Police Department, and the Washington, D.C., Metropolitan Police Department. Obviously, the number of cases is too few to permit any statistical analysis. Instead, we sought some specifics—across police departments that varied widely in size, threat perception, and other characteristics—that would make the survey results more vivid. In addition, we use the case study sites to highlight issues that may emerge in the future as LEAs continue to shape and refine their intelligence activities.

Chapter Four asks about the authorizing environment in which state and local LEAs conduct their intelligence activities. How have courts responded? What guidelines are in place? How are states reshaping their wiretap and other surveillance authorities? The chapter concludes with an "ideal" pattern or division of labor among the levels of government in the intelligence war on terrorism and offers suggestions about what actions are needed to move toward that ideal.

Finally, Chapter Five pulls together the lessons and issues from the preceding chapters and identifies some issues that LEAs will confront in the future.

A final note: This report focuses on LEA involvement in intelligence activities designed to counter terrorist actions. These activities may range from investigation of possible criminal acts (by means of electronic surveillance) to data collection that is incident to the normal activities of LEA officers but that is divorced from any specific criminal case. These activities may be carried out collaboratively with other agencies. Any discussion of nonintelligence measures, perceptions, and activities is provided primarily for context. Our focus is on intelligence activities at the state and local level.

The Response of Law Enforcement to 9/11: Survey Results

In this chapter we present selected results about law enforcement's intelligence function from a 2002 RAND survey.[1] The chapter begins with a brief description of the survey methodology and then presents the following results with respect to state and local law enforcement:

- Prior experience with terrorism-related incidents
- Formation of specialized terrorism units
- Coordination and information-sharing activities
- Assessment activities
- Support needs.

Methods

The survey targeted a stratified, random sample of 209 local law enforcement agencies and a census of the 50 state law enforcement agencies in the United States. The stratified, random sample represents nearly 18,000 law enforcement agencies nationwide, including the approximately 1,000 with at least 100 full-time sworn officers (BJS, 2002). The sample of local law enforcement agencies was designed to achieve geographic representation, as well as county size and departmental size representation. Overall, a high response rate was achieved for both groups (Table 2.1).

---

[1] The complete survey and analysis can be found in Davis et al. (2004).

Table 2.1
Survey Sample and Response Rates

	Number of Organizations Surveyed	Number of Organizations Responding	Response Rate
Local law enforcement	209[a]	169	81%
State law enforcement	50	39	78%

[a] Two counties were ineligible for the survey.

The mail survey of law enforcement agencies collected information on threat environment and organizational experience, departmental resources before 9/11, emergency response planning activities, and organizational information. Results from the descriptive analyses are presented below. For the local law enforcement sample, we calculated survey weights to take into account differences in each local law enforcement agency's probability of being selected into the sample and for nonresponses. The results for local law enforcement are weighted to be representative of the nation. For state law enforcement organizations, no weighting was necessary because we undertook a census of these organizations. We used a finite population correction in deriving the standard errors for these state-level organizations.

Although the survey is intended to be representative of law enforcement roles in countering terrorism, there are three caveats to our study. First, the study focus is on organizations. Thus, the responses depend on how informed a particular individual is about his or her organization's experiences with terrorism-related incidents and preparedness activities. To the extent that individuals who completed the survey for their organization differed in their level of knowledge about their organization's experience in this area, the responses received may partly reflect true differences among organizations and partly reflect differences in knowledge and experience of respondents about their organization. Second, although we investigated systematic nonresponse (along such sample selection dimensions as size of force, population, and so forth), nonrespondents may still differ from respondents in ways that we could not detect. Finally, the roles and responsibilities of state law enforcement agencies vary considerably from state to state. Thus, it is important to keep in mind that these organizations may serve different functions, including with respect to terrorism preparedness. We do not believe these issues unduly limit the utility or scientific credibility of our findings.

Survey Results

Prior Experience with Terrorism-Related Incidents

State and local law enforcement agencies were asked what types of terrorist groups were located within their state or jurisdiction. Substantial majorities of state law enforcement agencies indicated knowledge of terrorist groups within their state, but much smaller minorities of local law enforcement agencies indicated knowledge of such groups operating in their jurisdiction (Table 2.2).

Most local law enforcement agencies (88 percent) indicated that no incidents attributed to a terrorist group had occurred within their jurisdiction within the past five years (Table 2.3). In terms of frequency of occurrence, only one out of ten local law enforcement agencies reported that 1–5 such incidents had occurred in their jurisdiction during this time period, suggesting that prior experience at the local level with terrorist-related incidents has been very low.

In comparison, state law enforcement agencies tended to have greater awareness of, and experience with, such incidents. Most state

Table 2.2
Reported Terrorist Groups Located Within Jurisdiction (%)

Type of Group	All State LEAs	All Local LEAs
Right-wing groups	85 (3)	17 (5)
Race/ethnicity/hate-related groups	82 (3)	19 (6)
Religious groups using violence	38 (4)	3 (1)
Single issue/special interest groups	74 (3)	24 (7)
Millennial/doomsday cults	8 (2)	3 (3)
Other	15 (3)	7 (4)

NOTE: Standard errors are in parentheses.

Table 2.3
Reported Frequency of Incidents in Past Five
Years Attributed to Terrorist Group(s)

No. of Incidents	Within Their State, % of All State LEAs	Within Their Jurisdiction, % of All Local LEAs
None	32 (8)	88 (4)
1–5	35 (8)	10 (4)
6–10	14 (6)	1 (.5)
11–15	8 (4)	0.4 (.2)
16–20	3 (3)	0.1 (.1)
Over 21	8 (4)	0.4 (.4)

NOTE: Standard errors are in parentheses.

law enforcement agencies indicated at least one incident attributed to a terrorist group had occurred within their state during the past five years; only a third reported that no such incidents had occurred (see Table 2.3). In addition, states reported more of such incidents. One-third of state agencies reported 1–5 occurrences in the past five years; 14 percent reported 6–10 incidents; and 8 percent reported 11–15 incidents. Another 8 percent of agencies indicated that more than 21 such incidents had occurred within their state during this time period.

In addition, many state law enforcement agencies reported having been involved in the investigation of a terrorist-related incident prior to 9/11, compared to only 13 percent of local law enforcement agencies (Table 2.4). Other ways in which state law enforcement agencies were involved in terrorist-related incidents included providing information in support of an investigation (69 percent), surveillance activities (54 percent), and assisting with the collection of evidence (38 percent). In contrast, for the few local law enforcement agencies that indicated that had been involved with such incidents prior to 9/11, the involvement was primarily limited to assisting with an investigation or providing information.

Following 9/11, nearly all state law enforcement agencies, but only 42 percent of local law enforcement agencies, indicated that they

Table 2.4
Law Enforcement Involvement in Terrorist-Related Incident(s)
Prior to 9/11 (%)

Type of Involvement	All State LEAs	All Local LEAs
Investigation	64 (8)	13 (5)
Surveillance	54 (8)	6 (2)
Asked to provide information	69 (7)	12 (3)
Placed on alert	46 (8)	12 (4)
Prosecution	23 (7)	2 (1)
Collection of evidence	38 (8)	4 (1)
Scientific analysis	23 (7)	2 (1)
Other	13 (5)	2 (1)

NOTES: Respondents were asked to mark all categories that applied.
Standard errors are in parentheses.

experienced a terrorist-related hoax or incident that required a response by their department (Table 2.5). Large local law enforcement agencies (those with 101 or more sworn personnel) were almost twice as likely to report having experienced such hoaxes or incidents following 9/11 than other law enforcement agencies.

Table 2.5
LEAs Experiencing Terrorist-Related Hoaxes
or Incidents Following 9/11 That Required
Response (% of all LEAs)

	Yes, Experienced Hoaxes or Incidents
State LEAs	90 (2)
Local LEAs	
Overall	42 (10)
By department size	
0–30 officers	40 (14)
31–100 officers	38 (12)
101+ officers	79 (8)

NOTE: Standard errors are in parentheses.

Specialized Terrorism Units

Relatively few local law enforcement agencies (16 percent) reported having a specialized terrorism unit[2] (Table 2.6), and only 10 percent indicated they had a criminal intelligence unit. In contrast, 49 percent of local law enforcement agencies reported having a narcotics unit, 9 percent had gang abatement units, 8 percent had white-collar crime units, 6 percent had hate crime units, 4 percent had organized crime units, and 17 percent had other types of units (e.g., SWAT teams, bomb squads, domestic violence units, drug task forces, or computer crime units). The prevalence of drug units is a function of the historical priority placed on combating drug crimes and the federal support available for such efforts.[3]

In comparison, three-quarters of state law enforcement agencies reported having a specialized terrorism unit and 64 percent indicated also having a separate intelligence unit (not shown). The responsibilities of the state law enforcement agencies' terrorism units were broader than those of local law enforcement agencies. Whereas local agencies' terrorism units primarily were responsible for liaison, intelligence gathering, and analysis and dissemination of information, state law enforcement agencies' terrorism units were also involved in training of other law enforcement personnel and in investigating incidents.

Of those local law enforcement agencies with a specialized terrorism unit, the majority (79 percent) indicated that their unit had participated in joint training exercises following 9/11, primarily with other city or county agencies (Table 2.7). Of state law enforcement agencies with a specialized terrorism unit, nearly all said their units

---

[2] Survey respondents were asked if their department had a specialized unit, section, group, or individual(s) specifically assigned responsibility for addressing terrorism.

[3] On this topic, see http://www.whitehousedrugpolicy.gov/hidta/ for an overview of the federal High Intensity Drug Trafficking Areas (HIDTA) program of the Office of National Drug Control Policy.

Table 2.6
Law Enforcement Agencies with a Specialized Terrorism Unit (%)

Have Specialized Unit/Section/Group?	All State LEAs	All Local LEAs
Yes	77 (3)	16 (5)

	State LEAs with a specialized unit	Local LEAs with a specialized unit
What are its duties?		
Liaise with other law enforcement agencies	90 (4)	97 (2)
Gather intelligence	83 (4)	88 (5)
Analyze and disseminate information	87 (4)	60 (13)
Liaise with federal agencies	90 (4)	51 (13)
Provide intelligence information to other law enforcement agencies	87 (4)	50 (13)
Train other law enforcement personnel or agencies	57 (6)	38 (13)
Provide resources to other LEAs	50 (6)	28 (9)
Investigate specific terrorist incidents	67 (6)	15 (5)

NOTE: Standard errors are in parentheses.

had participated since 9/11 in joint training exercises with a variety of entities, especially with other state agencies and the FBI.

One issue that the survey did not capture was the prevalence of local prohibitions on forming intelligence groups. Measuring the extent to which such prohibitions exist and the degree to which they are enforced is difficult. Anecdotally, there are examples of such opposition. Recently, the Portland (Oregon) City Council, acting on a recommendation from its mayor, withdrew the police from the FBI

Table 2.7
Law Enforcement Agencies with Specialized Terrorism
Units Participating in Joint Training Exercises
Since 9/11 (%)

Participate in Joint Training Exercises Since 9/11?	State LEAs	Local LEAs
Yes	90 (6)	79 (8)
If so, with whom?		
Other city or county agencies	43 (9)	66 (10)
State agencies (in state)	77 (8)	34 (12)
State agencies (out of state)	33 (9)	6 (4)
FBI	53 (9)	29 (10)
U.S. Secret Service	10 (6)	3 (2)
U.S. Drug Enforcement Administration	10 (6)	6 (5)
Professional or fraternal associations; informal working groups	20 (7)	7 (3)

NOTE: Standard errors are in parentheses.

JTTF primarily because the FBI would not grant the mayor the secret security clearance he felt he needed to supervise the cases properly.[4]

Similarly, several states quit the Multistate Antiterrorism Information Exchange, known as MATRIX, out of concerns that included protection of privacy and the social impact of interstate data sharing.[5] Although MATRIX did not have intelligence gathering functions but focused instead on enabling information sharing across state lines, opposition to the program was substantial. Program officials report that the MATRIX pilot was completed on April 15, 2005.[6] Still other

---

[4] *Seattle Post-Intelligencer*, "Portland Becomes First to Pull Out of FBI-Led Anti-Terror Team," April 29, 2005. Available at http://seattlepi.nwsource.com/local/222207_fbi29.html, accessed on May 23, 2005.

[5] See, for example, *Information Week*, "Two More States Withdraw from Database Program," March 12, 2004. Available at http://www.informationweek.com/story/showArticle. jhtml?articleID=18312112, accessed on May 23, 2005.

[6] According to the MATRIX site, www.matrix-at.org/, "This web site will be available until July 1, 2005 as a courtesy, but will be discontinued after that date."

elected municipal officials, such as the City Council in Ann Arbor, Mich., have expressed opposition to perceived excesses of intelligence activities while leaving their intelligence authorities largely intact. Among other actions, the Ann Arbor City Council directed the Chief of Police to

> [r]efrain from participating in informational interviews . . . conducted by the Federal Bureau of Investigation (FBI) . . . of individuals not suspected of criminal activity" and "[c]ontinue to refrain from covert surveillance of and/or collection and maintenance of information on individuals or groups based on their participation in activities protected by the First Amendment, such as political advocacy or the practice of a religion, without a particularized suspicion of unlawful activity.[7]

Coordination on Intelligence Information-Sharing and Investigations

Prior to 9/11, the FBI had established JTTFs[8] in many field offices. Composed of teams of state and local law enforcement agencies, FBI agents, and representatives of other federal agencies,[9] the JTTFs are intended to facilitate cooperation to prevent terrorist attacks and to share information on investigations (GAO, 2003). Following the 9/11 attacks, the FBI increased the number of JTTFs from 36 in 2001 to 84 JTTFs in 2003 (Office of the Inspector General, 2003).

One year following the 9/11 attacks, only a third of local law enforcement agencies reported interacting with the FBI's JTTFs, primarily to share intelligence information or to receive counter-

---

[7] Both quotes are from "Resolution to Protest the Eroding of Civil Liberties Under the USA Patriot Act (Public Law 107-56) and Related Federal Orders Since 9/11/01" approved by the Ann Arbor City Council on July 7, 2003. Available at http://justpeaceinfo.org/res-aa-cc-7july2003.html, accessed on May 23, 2005.

[8] The JTTFs vary in size and structure in relation to the terrorist threat dealt with by each FBI field office. On average, 40 to 50 people are assigned full-time to the JTTFs; however, some task forces, such as that in New York City, can have as many as 550 personnel, and a number of part-time personnel can also be assigned to the JTTFs (Office of the Inspector General, 2003).

[9] Federal Bureau of Investigation War on Terrorism, http://www.fbi.gov/terrorinfo/counterrorism/waronterrorhome.htm, accessed on September 7, 2005.

terrorism training (Table 2.8). In comparison, most state law enforcement agencies reported having interacted with the FBI's JTTFs during the past five years. Of those that did, the primary reasons were to share intelligence on the terrorist threat or to provide assistance with an investigation. Unlike local law enforcement, few state law enforcement agencies had received counterterrorism training from the FBI, suggesting that at the state-level law enforcement agencies may be receiving this training from other sources.[10]

Table 2.8
Coordination with FBI's Joint Terrorism Task Forces (%)

Coordinated with the FBI's JTTFs?	All State LEAs	All Local LEAs
Yes	95 (2)	36 (9)
	State LEAs That Coordinated	**Local LEAs That Coordinated**
If so, for what purpose?		
Assist with investigation	41 (4)	17 (6)
Share intelligence information	68 (4)	64 (11)
Receive counterterrorism training	24 (4)	44 (11)
Other purposes	24 (4)	6 (3)

NOTES: The purposes for which agencies have interacted with the FBI's JTTFs represent a lower-bound estimate for each category. Respondents were asked to check only one answer. Of the 112 local law enforcement agencies that answered this question, 83 followed instructions and checked one category only; 29 checked multiple categories. Of the 37 state law enforcement agencies that answered this question, 23 followed instructions and checked one category only; 14 checked multiple categories. For each group, we report the combined results in the table. Standard errors are in parentheses.

---

[10] A number of federal agencies and private and nonprofit organizations provide counterterrorism training. As a result, the Department of Justice (DOJ) created the Counterterrorism Training and Resources for Law Enforcement portal Web site, which is intended to serve as a single point of access on counterterrorism training opportunities and related materials. See http://www.counterterrorismtraining.gov/mission/index.html.

Although not shown, approximately three-quarters of state law enforcement agencies and two-thirds of local law enforcement agencies indicated they had received guidance from the FBI following the 9/11 attacks as to what type of information they should collect and pass on to the field offices or to the JTTFs.

With respect to interagency task forces, 42 percent of local law enforcement agencies said they either formally liased with or were an official member of at least one terrorism-related task force (Table 2.9). They primarily were linked to city/county interagency task forces or the Attorney General's anti-terrorism task force (ATTF) of their state. Thirty-six percent of local law enforcement agencies also reported participating with the JTTFs. In terms of training, one-third of the local law enforcement agencies that were linked to at least one terrorism-related task force reported participating on an ad hoc basis in tabletop or field exercises with these task forces (particularly with the city/county interagency task force) (not shown).

Table 2.9
Law Enforcement Agency Participation in Terrorism-Related Task Forces (%)

Liaise with or Member of Task Force?	All State LEAs	All Local LEAs
Yes	90 (2)	42 (11)

	State LEAs That Liaised with or Were Members	Local LEAs That Liaised with or Were Members
If so, with which ones(s)?		
FBI's JTTFs	89 (3)	36 (9)
State ATTFs	77 (4)	44 (11)
State homeland security office task force	77 (4)	23 (8)
City/county task forces	20 (4)	42 (10)
Other task force(s)	17 (4)	10 (10)

NOTE: Standard errors are in parentheses.

In comparison, nearly all state law enforcement agencies either formally liased with or were an official member of at least one terrorism-related task force. At the federal level, they liaised with the JTTFs; at the state level, with the ATTFs or their state's homeland security office task force. One out of five state law enforcement agencies also liaised with city or county interagency task forces. Participation in field or tabletop exercises with these task forces was primarily done on an ad hoc basis (not shown).

Information Sources That Law Enforcement Agencies Rely On
What information sources do LEAs rely on? Table 2.10 indicates which information sources about terrorism or the terrorist threat that *local law enforcement agencies* use.[11] Law enforcement agencies were asked to mark one answer per row, indicating if they never used that information source or, if they did, to rate how useful it was to them.[12]

Approximately 45–50 percent of local law enforcement agencies considered information received from the internet and from their state's office of homeland security and state's U.S. Attorney General's ATTF to be somewhat useful sources. More local law enforcement agencies (approximately two-thirds) considered the FBI's unclassified reports to be somewhat useful information sources, along with information received from other federal agencies, professional law enforcement publications, and from other state agencies and local jurisdictions. Approximately 20 percent of local law enforcement agencies rated information about the terrorist threat received from the FBI's JTTFs as being very useful to their agency. Smaller percentages described their state ATTF and professional law enforcement publications as very useful.

In terms of information sources that were not relied upon, about two-thirds of local law enforcement respondents said their agency

---

[11] At the time of the survey in 2002, the FBI was introducing some new procedures, which were too new to be included in the survey.

[12] Thus, these responses may point out either that the information is not useful to the respondents or that respondents do not understand the value of the information.

Table 2.10
Perceived Utility of Information Sources Used by Local Law Enforcement
Agencies (%)

Information Source	Never Used	Not At All Useful	Somewhat Useful	Very Useful
FBI classified reports	51 (12)	1 (1)	32 (9)	15 (6)
FBI unclassified reports	22 (8)	4 (2)	66 (10)	8 (4)
FBI JTTFs	54 (11)	5 (3)	21 (7)	20 (7)
Other federal agencies	19 (8)	9 (5)	63 (10)	9 (5)
Your state's office of homeland security	25 (9)	17 (8)	44 (13)	13 (6)
Your state's ATTF	29 (9)	10 (6)	45 (13)	17 (7)
Other state agencies	20 (8)	10 (5)	57 (11)	13 (5)
Other local jurisdictions	24 (9)	6 (4)	55 (11)	15 (6)
Law enforcement professional association	27 (9)	18 (8)	34 (7)	21 (8)
Risk assessment services or publications	48 (13)	15 (7)	36 (10)	1 (1)
Internet	37 (14)	8 (4)	49 (12)	5 (2)
Media (electronic, print)	44 (13)	16 (6)	33 (9)	7 (5)
Professional law enforcement publications	30 (15)	5 (3)	60 (13)	5 (3)
Non–law enforcement books, journals, periodicals	49 (12)	19 (7)	31 (9)	1 (0.5)
Radical publications, other "alternative" literature	66 (9)	13 (5)	21 (6)	1 (0.3)

NOTES: Respondents were asked to mark only one box for each row. Standard errors are in parentheses.

never relied on radical publications or other "alternative" literature sources. Approximately half said their agency did not use FBI classified reports or information from the FBI's JTTFs. Approximately 45–50 percent indicated that their agency never used information from the media; risk assessment services; or journals, periodicals, or books not related to law enforcement.

Table 2.11 indicates which information sources about terrorism or the terrorist threat that state law enforcement agencies use and

Table 2.11
Perceived Utility of Information Sources Used by State Law Enforcement Agencies (%)

Information Sources	Never Used	Not At All Useful	Somewhat Useful	Very Useful
FBI classified reports	21 (3)	3 (1)	51 (4)	26 (3)
FBI unclassified reports	3 (1)	3 (1)	79 (3)	15 (3)
FBI JTTFs	3 (1)	8 (2)	51 (4)	38 (4)
Other federal agencies	0	0	74 (3)	26 (3)
Your state's office of homeland security	8 (2)	22 (3)	35 (4)	35 (4)
Your state's ATTF	13 (3)	5 (2)	59 (4)	23 (3)
Other state agencies	3 (1)	8 (2)	54 (4)	36 (4)
Other local jurisdictions	5 (2)	10 (2)	64 (4)	21 (3)
Law enforcement professional association	13 (3)	18 (3)	56 (4)	13 (3)
Risk assessment services or publications	26 (3)	16 (3)	53 (4)	5 (2)
Internet	10 (2)	5 (2)	54 (4)	31 (4)
Media (electronic, print)	5 (2)	15 (3)	62 (4)	18 (3)
Professional law enforcement publications	5 (2)	10 (2)	74 (3)	10 (2)
Books, journals, periodicals (non–law enforcement)	10 (2)	8 (2)	72 (3)	10 (2)
Radical publications; other "alternative" literature	26 (3)	5 (2)	53 (4)	16 (3)

NOTES: Respondents were asked to mark only one box for each row. Standard errors are in parentheses.

their ratings regarding the utility of those sources. In general, state law enforcement agencies used a greater variety of information sources than local law enforcement and tended to rate more of those sources as somewhat or very useful. Specifically, approximately 75–80 percent of state law enforcement agencies said they found somewhat useful the FBI unclassified reports and information received from other federal agencies, as well as information available in professional law enforcement and non–law enforcement publications. Very few state law enforcement agencies indicated they never used the information sources listed in Table 2.11. Only a quarter of state agencies indicated that they never used FBI classified reports, risk assessment services or publications, and radical publications or other alternative literature.

Approximately two-thirds of state law enforcement agencies also considered somewhat useful information obtained from their state's ATTF, the media, and from local jurisdictions. In addition, about half of state law enforcement agencies found somewhat useful information obtained from FBI classified reports and the FBI's JTTFs, from other state agencies, law enforcement professional associations, risk assessment services or publications, the internet and from radical publications or other "alternative" literature. About a third of agencies rated as being very useful information on the terrorist threat that they received from the FBI's JTTFs, their state's office of homeland security and from other state agencies, as well as from the internet.

Assessment Activities

Most state and local law enforcement agencies conducted a risk or threat assessment either in the year prior to the 9/11 attacks or during the year following the 9/11 attacks (Table 2.12). State law enforcement agencies tended to be more proactive than local law enforcement in this area prior to the 9/11 terrorist attacks. Whereas 44 percent of state law enforcement agencies indicated having conducted an assessment prior to 9/11, only 30 percent of local law enforcement agencies had done so. Approximately the same percentage of state agencies conducted an assessment following 9/11. Although not shown, an additional 9 percent of state law enforcement agencies indicated they had conducted an assessment both before and after 9/11.

In comparison, local law enforcement worked to catch up in doing assessments following the 9/11 attacks, with 68 percent indicating they had done so in the year after 9/11.[13] For both state and local law enforcement, the responsibility for conducting the assessment(s) fell upon their department or an interagency task force (not shown).

---

[13] Similar results for municipalities are found in Riley and Hoffman (1995).

Table 2.12
Execution of Risk or Threat Assessments (%)

Conducted Assessment?	All State LEAs	All Local LEAs
Yes	82 (3)	73 (8)

	State LEAs That Conducted Assessment	Local LEAs That Conducted Assessment
If so, when was it conducted?		
During the year before 9/11	44 (5)	30 (11)
During the year after 9/11	41 (5)	68 (11)

NOTE: Standard errors are in parentheses.

Table 2.13 shows the risk assessment results for local law enforcement by department size. Most of the large departments (101+ officers) indicated they had conducted a risk or threat assessment, with 41 percent having done so in the year prior to the 9/11 attacks. In comparison, only a third or less of the small (0–30 officers) and medium-sized (31–100 officers) departments had conducted an assessment before 9/11. However, these agencies then worked to catch up in their assessment activities after 9/11.

State law enforcement agencies' assessments tended to be broader in scope than those of local agencies—addressing key infrastructure, public buildings, government or military facilities, as well as their own department (Table 2.14). In part, this may be a reflection of broader state jurisdiction and the fact that state entities typically do not have to respond to citizen calls for service. In comparison, local law enforcement agencies focused primarily on key infrastructure and public buildings; only half indicated the assessment included their department and only a third said their assessment included government or military facilities.[14]

---

[14] A significant amount of national infrastructure is in private hands. For more on the role of the private sector in risk assessment and infrastructure protection, see *Executive Order on Critical Infrastructure Protection*, 2001, and Personick and Patterson, 2003.

Table 2.13
Local LEAs' Execution of Risk or Threat Assessments,
by Department Size (%)

Conducted Assessment?	Size of Department		
	0–30 Officers	31–100 Officers	101+ Officers
Yes	70 (12)	79 (10)	92 (4)
If so, when was it conducted?			
During the year before 9/11	33 (17)	19 (8)	41 (10)
During the year after 9/11	67 (17)	75 (10)	50 (11)

NOTE: Standard errors are in parentheses.

Table 2.14
Elements of Law Enforcement Agency
Assessments (%)

Assessment Focus	State LEAs	Local LEAs
Key public buildings	85 (4)	89 (6)
Key infrastructure (power, water, electricity, etc.)	93 (3)	73 (19)
Own department	81 (5)	51 (15)
Government or military facilities	85 (4)	37 (12)
Chemical plants	63 (6)	26 (11)
Agricultural facilities	44 (6)	17 (8)
Food processing/ packing plants	37 (6)	13 (7)
Other private businesses	37 (6)	27 (10)
Other	22 (5)	19 (9)

NOTES: Respondents were asked to mark all that apply.
Standard errors are in parentheses.

Nearly all large- and medium-sized local police departments have within their jurisdiction at least one major facility type that might be considered a potential terrorist target. Even smaller law enforcement agencies might be called on to respond to a terrorist-related incident in the future, with half indicating that their jurisdiction had at least one of the facility types listed in Table 2.15.

Table 2.15
Perceptions of Potential Terrorist Targets in
Local Jurisdiction, by Department Size

Yes, at Least One Potential Target	% of All Local LEAs
Overall	66 (13)
By department size	
0–30 officers	54 (16)
31–100 officers	91 (6)
101+ officers	94 (3)

NOTES: Facility types used to create this indicator included nuclear power plants or Department of Energy
nuclear facilities, weapons manufacturer or storage
facilities, chemical plants, water treatment plants,
hydroelectric dams, major port facilities, airports, major sports arenas or venues, or major suspension/
arterial bridges. Standard errors are in parentheses.

Intelligence Information About the Terrorist Threat

We asked survey respondents what type of support they needed to
improve their response capabilities. Sixty-four percent of state law
enforcement and 42 percent of local law enforcement agencies indicated a need for more and better intelligence information on the
threats facing their state or jurisdiction and on terrorist activity
within their region (Table 2.16). In addition, most state law enforcement agencies wanted more manpower to dedicate to counterterrorism activities and response planning, whereas only about one-
third of local law enforcement agencies indicated such a need. Nearly
half of state law enforcement agencies also wanted more intelligence
on terrorist threats and capabilities, while only 17 percent of local law
enforcement cited this as an important need.

In summer 2003, RAND conducted a nationwide survey of local law enforcement, fire service, state and local offices of emergency
management, state and local emergency medical services, hospitals,
and state and local public health organizations to gather information
on their views regarding federal preparedness programs for combating

Table 2.16
Intelligence and Information-Related Support Needs (%)

	All State LEAs	All Local LEAs
What Do You Need to Improve Response Capabilities?		
More/better intelligence information on threats and terrorist activity in region	64 (4)	42 (10)
More manpower dedicated to response planning and/or to counterterrorism activities	87 (3)	35 (9)
	Of LEAs That Indicated a Need for Some Type of Support . . .	
What Do You Need to Improve Assessment Capabilities?		
Better intelligence on terrorist threat/capability from federal government	47 (6)	17 (7)

NOTE: Standard errors are in parentheses.

terrorism (Davis et al., 2003). The survey was conducted in support of the Advisory Panel to Assess Domestic Response Capabilities for Terrorism Involving Weapons of Mass Destruction ("Gilmore Commission"). This more recent survey provides an additional perspective on state and local LEA information needs.

For instance, the 2003 survey found that both state and local organizations were looking to the Department of Homeland Security (DHS) for intelligence information and information about the terrorist threat within their jurisdiction or state. Sixty-two percent of local LEAs wanted more such information (Davis et al., 2003). In addition, among suggestions for improving the Homeland Advisory System, 60–70 percent of state and local organizations wanted the system to provide additional information about the threat (type of incident likely to occur, where the threat is likely to occur, and during what time period) to help guide them in responding to changes in the threat level. Other suggestions for improving the Homeland Advisory System included (1) using a regional or sectoral alert system to notify emergency responders about threats specific to their jurisdiction/state,[15] (2) providing training to emergency responders about what protective actions are necessary at different threat levels, and (3) after an increase in threat level, having DHS follow up on what additional actions ought to be taken.[16]

Despite a desire for more detailed intelligence information, few local LEAs were in a position to receive it. Only 7 percent of local agencies indicated having applied for security clearances for their personnel since 9/11 (Davis et al., 2003, Table 7E). Of those that had applied, only half indicated that all their personnel who had applied had received their clearances.[17] State offices of emergency management and state public health departments were more likely than LEAs to have sought security clearances for their personnel since the 9/11 attacks.[18] Because the survey did not ask when organizations had applied for government security clearances, it was not clear how long the waiting times are for clearances. Still, the mismatch between the desire for more intelligence information and the ability to receive it is striking.

---

[15] At this writing, the Homeland Security Advisory System of color-coded alerts is still national in scope. However, it appears to be increasingly used to raise the alert level for specific industry sectors. For example, in the aftermath of the London rail attacks, DHS raised the alert level to orange for the mass transit sector and left it at yellow for the rest of the nation.

[16] Between 60 and 70 percent of state and local organizations listed these additional recommendations for improving the advisory system.

[17] The relatively low percentage of agencies applying for security clearances may be a function of the fact that most law enforcement agencies are very small and thus may have limited need for sensitive material or a limited ability to use it. The relatively slow rate of granting security clearances is likely a function of a post-9/11 surge in demand for what is already a lengthy and detailed process. See Davis et al., 2003.

[18] DHS announced in April 2003 that in addition to the state governors, five senior officials within each state would be issued security clearances to receive classified information and to allow governors to obtain intelligence information that federal agencies may have about specific threats or targets. These clearances are in addition to the security clearances to be issued to public health officials (DHS, 2003).

What Does the Survey Tell Us?

The 2002 survey raises some key points about state and local LEAs and counterterrorism intelligence. The first is that many such agencies, particularly local ones, lack experience with and exposure to terrorism issues. Typically, they have not responded to incidents, are less likely to claim that there are radical groups operating in their jurisdiction, and less likely to operate specialized groups or functions.

The survey findings tend to belie the notion that counterterrorism intelligence is a pervasive function among LEAs. Instead, the survey findings, which reflect heightened awareness associated with the Oklahoma City and September 11 attacks, suggest that the "eyes and ears" capability is concentrated among the larger departments. These are the agencies investing in training, response plans, coordination, and other preparedness measures. This in turn suggests that the process of shaping and directing state and local LEA involvement in intelligence activities may be narrower and more focused than previously thought.

What the survey does not reveal is how the larger departments and agencies are organizing, resourcing, and conducting their intelligence efforts. Similarly, the survey—which was fielded three years ago—does not tell us much about the current state of affairs. The field of intelligence is dynamic and fast moving and a survey conducted in 2002 cannot provide insight into the contemporary dimensions of the issue. However, the survey does provide a benchmark against which the impact of future changes or deviations can be measured. More important, the survey provided insights into the types of issues that we addressed through the cases studies. For the operational detail, we turn to case studies of eight agencies across the United States.

CHAPTER THREE

Organizing for Intelligence: Case Studies of Law Enforcement Agencies

The survey results presented in Chapter Two offer an overall picture of how local and state police agencies have responded to changing demands resulting from an enhanced terrorist threat arising from the September 11, 2001, terrorist attacks. To complement this insight, we sought to gain a more in-depth look at recent changes in specific agencies by interviewing key respondents who were knowledgeable about counterterrorism intelligence operations in their organizations.

In all, we studied eight police organizations: Charlotte-Mecklenberg (N.C.) Police Department (CMPD), Columbus (Ohio) Division of Police (CDP), Fairfax County (Va.) Police Department (FCPD), Las Vegas Metropolitan Police Department (LVMPD), Los Angeles Police Department (LAPD), Oakland Police Department (OPD), San Diego Police Department (SDPD), and Washington, D.C., Metropolitan Police Department (WDCMPD). During March through July of 2004, we interviewed respondents from these agencies' command staffs who were familiar with agency intelligence operations. We chose these agencies because they were developing, or already possessed, an intelligence capability. As such, our case study sample is not intended to be representative. Rather, it provided a more detailed picture of organizations that are developing or operating intelligence functions. Because of our selection method, we are unable to characterize agencies that have opted not to develop such capacity. Table 3.1 shows the case study LEAs and the components within the LEA that house the counterterrorism intelligence function.

Table 3.1
Units Responsible for Counterterrorism Intelligence, Case Study Sites

Organization	Unit
Charlotte-Mecklenberg Police Department	Criminal Intelligence Unit
Columbus Division of Police	Intelligence Bureau
Fairfax County Police Department	Criminal Investigations Bureau
Las Vegas Metropolitan Police Department	Homeland Security Bureau
Los Angeles Police Department	Counterterrorism and Criminal Intelligence Bureau
Oakland Police Department	Bureau of Intelligence
San Diego Police Department	Criminal Intelligence Unit
Washington, D.C., Metropolitan Police Department	Special Services Command

It is important to acknowledge that these cases are in no way a representative sample of local police agencies. The number of agencies is quite small, and they were not randomly chosen. Although the agencies varied in geographic location and size, they were limited to those willing to participate in this study. These factors reduce the extent to which the experiences of these police agencies can be generalized to other agencies. However, the objective of the case studies is to illustrate the breadth of responses and changes in local police functions caused by increased concerns about terrorism, not to provide a complete account.

As with the surveys, the cases rely almost exclusively on the information provided by a single or a few individuals in each organization. The validity of the information thus depends on the extent to which the respondents know what is going on in their organizations. We sought to minimize this source of bias by interviewing respondents who were most informed about the counterterrorism intelligence function of their organization.

The remaining sections of this chapter are organized around six thematic areas: intelligence mandate and guidelines; oversight; counterterrorism structure, tasks, and costs; personnel and training; information sources; and communication within and among agencies. Each of these thematic areas was addressed in the survey.

Mandate and Guidelines

Since 9/11, there has been considerable rethinking of what the counterterrorism function for local law enforcement agencies should be and who should determine it. In the local police agencies we studied, the mandate of most intelligence units conducting counterterrorism functions is fairly informal and broad and is usually defined by oral, not written, guidelines.

Respondents summarized the mandates of their counterterrorism activities in the following terms:

- Update crime and gang intelligence, facilitate counterterrorism partnerships with federal agencies, and facilitate the day-to-day ability to operate.
- Keep the chief apprised of crime issues, such as gangs, terrorism, drugs, local anarchy, and organized crime, that may not get to him through normal channels.
- Support officers on patrol—give them information to perform their job safely.

The counterterrorism mandate of most agencies we examined is set internally, either by the command staff or the chief. In one agency that has a small number of personnel devoted to counterterrorism efforts, the FBI sets the mandate through the agency's participation on the JTTF. A board of police commissioners determines LAPD's mandate, as well as the department's broader standards and procedures (S&P). That mandate is formally documented in the S&P. It describes the objectives as preventing terrorist activity in Los Angeles and the surrounding area, advising the chief and executive management about pending events that may require planning or police service, and ensuring the safety of persons and protection of property through intelligence gathering and collaboration with other agencies.

The local LEAs vary in how they codify and apply formal guidelines to counterterrorism intelligence collection, use, dissemination, and retention. While they generally acknowledge following the federal regulations, some, but not all, have developed their own guidelines to complement the federal regulations or are in the process of doing so.[1] LAPD provides a rich history of guideline development. During the 1960s, LAPD created an official intelligence function that focused on public disorder, organized crime, demonstrators, and violent groups such as the Mafia and the Black Panthers. LAPD's undercover operations spawned several lawsuits in the late 1970s and early 1980s. In 1982, it reached a settlement with the American Civil Liberties Union that required it to create written standards and procedures for intelligence and crime investigation related to terrorism. The Police Commission formally approved the first set of guidelines in 1984, and the guidelines have been amended several times since (the last time being March 18, 2003). Coinciding with the codification of the S&P was a reorganization that split organized crime and antiterrorism (now called "major crimes") into two separate divisions.

LAPD's S&P have been changed in three main ways. First, the standard for opening a case—which had been "probable cause" after the lawsuits in the late 1970s—was regarded by LAPD as too high for effective intelligence gathering. After the Oklahoma City bombing on April 19, 1995, the standard for opening a case was reduced to "reasonable suspicion." Second, the S&P were rewritten to better articulate what constitutes reasonable suspicion (initial leads can be less than reasonable suspicion, as explained in the S&P).[2] Third, after the 9/11 attacks, the S&P were deemed to apply to intelligence only and

---

[1] The relevant federal guidelines are laid out in 28 CFR Part 23, which details standards for police agencies that implement federally funded multijurisdictional criminal intelligence systems. It provides guidance for entering information, security, inquiry, dissemination, review, and purge. See Institute for Intergovernmental Research, http://www.iir.com/28cfr/ Overview.htm, accessed May 23, 2005. The *National Criminal Intelligence Sharing Plan* recommends that all state and local intelligence systems adopt the standards of 28 CFR Part 23, regardless of whether the system is federally funded (BJA, 2003, p. 5).

[2] LAPD's S&P, approved March 18, 2003, define *reasonable suspicion* as "An honest belief based on known articulable circumstances which would cause a reasonable and trained law enforcement officer to believe that some activity relating to a definable criminal activity or enterprise may be occurring or has a potential to occur."

not criminal investigations.[3] A respondent explained that no other major changes occurred in LAPD's policy because the department already had infrastructure in place for intelligence gathering prior to the 9/11 attacks.

LVMPD also maintains written guidelines pertaining to intelligence, and it is in the process of rewriting them. The department has not differentiated between terrorism and criminal intelligence because it contends that they are legally no different. In addition to the federal guidelines, it currently abides by guidelines set forth by the Law Enforcement Intelligence Unit (LEIU), which is an organization created to share information and promote police intelligence. FCPD also follows LEIU guidelines, as well as the *National Criminal Intelligence Sharing Plan.*[4]

In other agencies, internal guidelines are more informal. One respondent candidly explained, "standard operating procedures should reflect guidelines for intelligence collection, retention, and dissemination, but we haven't done a great job in doing so. Issues are simply talked about as they come up."[5] When asked about the Patriot Act, one respondent advised that it has not impacted his agency's internal guidelines in any way.

It appears that local police primarily rely on federal regulations when it comes to counterterrorism intelligence gathering, and this has not changed much since the 9/11 terrorist attacks. However, the enhanced terrorist threat has increased awareness of these issues and has spurred review and development of internal guidelines in some local police organizations.

---

[3] An LAPD respondent advised that standards and procedures for intelligence gathering should be written and approved by civilian oversight or the function can be very dangerous. For example, if a police agency is sued over intelligence activities and there are no standards and procedures in place, the standards and procedures that will likely result from the lawsuit will be much more restrictive than if they had been created beforehand.

[4] The Global Justice Information Sharing Initiative Intelligence Working Group, which is a national criminal intelligence council, developed the *National Criminal Intelligence Sharing Plan.* The Executive Summary and other reference materials about the plan are available at http://it.ojp.gov/topic.jsp?topic_id=103, accessed September 8, 2005.

[5] Interview with a counterterrorism intelligence source, March 12, 2004.

Oversight

Given the increased need for enhanced information gathering, the oversight of that process and related police activity deserves attention. In order to protect civil liberties and personal privacy and reduce the potential for litigation, police agencies must be very careful about the way in which they conduct their intelligence function. In most agencies we examined, the primary mechanism for providing oversight of intelligence activities rests within the chain of command. That is, the police command staff have the responsibility for determining what should and will be done, and for reviewing ongoing cases. In CMPD for example, criminal intelligence supervisors and detectives assigned to the JTTF meet with the chief of police and selected command staff on a weekly basis to discuss terrorism issues.

Some local police agencies have supplemented the internal oversight of their intelligence functions with various forms of external oversight. For example, per LAPD's S&P, a civilian committee must approve all information gathering activities prior to undercover operation. This committee also conducts an oversight audit at least once a year, and it can review any intelligence activity at any time. Other LEAs utilize various external agencies for oversight and as consultants. WDCMPD shares information with the city council and attorneys, and OPD and CMPD work with federal agencies such as the FBI and Secret Service. Similar to LAPD, SDPD's files undergo a systematic review every quarter; the review is conducted by the city manager's office.

States and localities have access to a number of resources to help them structure, shape and refine their intelligence activities, including the *National Criminal Intelligence Sharing Plan* (BJA, 2003) and the *Law Enforcement Analytic Standards* (Global Justice Information Sharing Initiative, 2004). In some case studies (such as Los Angeles), it was evident that previous local experience with intelligence abuses was a driving factor.[6] Case study participants did not indicate the ex-

---

[6] For more insight into historic events in Los Angeles, see Wildhorn, Jenkins, and Lavin, 1982.

tent to which they relied on these or other resources to plan their local intelligence efforts. Likewise, case study participants did not identify any common authoritative source that they used to plan their efforts.

Structure, Tasks, and Costs

In general, local police agencies did not develop distinct organizational units in which to conduct their counterterrorism intelligence activities. Instead, those tasks are executed in conjunction with the intelligence activities pertaining to other major crimes. For example, the responsibility for counterterrorism in CDP, OPD, WDCMPD, and SDP rests primarily within an intelligence bureau or division. These general intelligence units are also responsible for such issues as gangs, organized crime, and economic crime. In LAPD, the major crimes division of the Critical Incident Management Bureau conducts terrorism investigation and prevention, functions performed by the criminal intelligence section of LVMPD's Homeland Security Bureau and the criminal intelligence unit of CMPD.

Of the eight case studies we conducted, only FCPD and LVMPD reported having made significant changes in their organizational structure after the 9/11 attacks. After 9/11, FCPD supplemented its Criminal Investigations Bureau with a criminal intelligence unit that focuses on terrorism and weapons of mass destruction. LVMPD initially had a criminal intelligence section, but in 2003 it created a Homeland Security Bureau. Among other sections, this new bureau includes criminal intelligence and operations sections. The criminal intelligence section conducts both criminal and terrorism intelligence functions. LVMPD noted the utility of pairing these functions because most intelligence for terrorism actually starts from criminal cases, such as credit card fraud. The operations section comprises detectives who follow up on patrol officer leads. If the leads are found to be terrorist related, they are reported to the FBI's JTTF. LVMPD sees these as two separate but related functions and contends that both use the same analytical process.

Although these local police agencies do not separate the counterterrorism intelligence function from other functions structurally, that is not to suggest they find no utility in differentiating the general intelligence tasks. All the agencies assign at least one member to the FBI's JTTF. Some local police distinguish intelligence gathering from analysis. CMPD and CDP, for instance, maintain permanently assigned intelligence analysts who review and assess intelligence information collected by others.

The cost of increasing the counterterrorism intelligence function has burdened some local law enforcement agencies. For instance, LAPD has increased expenditures on intelligence gathering but without new budget allocations. Funds have been shifted internally and the city has received some grants. As a respondent explained,

> There is a need for overtime with security level changes, but this is not budgeted. Most funding goes toward equipment, which wears out. There is a need for a long-term budget strategy that accounts for the leasing of space, equipment, and personnel. Most grants are of the payback form—spend the money and then receive reimbursement. One difficulty that arises is when money is available for equipment/systems, but none of it can be used for the operators and maintainers of the equipment/systems.[7]

It is apparent that some agencies are spending more to account for an increased threat level, which implies that the focus on counterterrorism will wane if new attacks do not occur. One respondent suggested that no new attacks would mean layoffs at his agency. For other LEAs, however, the shift in resources has been less marked, and so the impact has been less taxing. Federal grant funding has opened up for some agencies. CMPD, for instance, is sharing $7.4 million with other agencies in North Carolina and South Carolina for equipment purchases, alert teams, and training. It is not evident, however, that such grant funding can be used for actual intelligence gathering and analysis activities.

---

[7] Interview with a counterterrorism intelligence source, March 2, 2004.

Personnel and Training

The counterterrorism mission has affected at least two important personnel areas—investment in human resources for intelligence gathering and analysis, and training. Some agencies have increased their
human resource commitment to counterterrorism. For example, since
the 9/11 attacks, WDCMPD and LVMPD increased their numbers
of personnel devoted to counterterrorism intelligence by 10–15 percent and 50 percent, respectively. LAPD stands out in this regard,
having increased the number of personnel devoted to intelligence
fivefold.

It is important to know from where these increases came. For
the most part, the commitment of personnel to counterterrorism
came at the expense of other police tasks. These agencies have not
hired additional personnel but instead have had to pull officers from
assignments in such areas as patrol, gangs, narcotics, fraud and for-
gery, vice, burglary, and auto theft. In light of the terrorist threat,
some organizations have reprioritized their investment areas in favor
of counterterrorism—to the detriment of other crime areas. A possible exception to this is FCPD, which developed a specialty team of
about 15 highly trained auxiliary officers who were hand-selected for
intelligence gathering. This practice enhanced the overall counterterrorism capacity without unduly burdening other functional areas.

In spite of the enhanced terrorist threat, most agencies reported
little change in the amount and type of training offered to their intelligence staff. Some respondents believed their intelligence personnel
have all the training they need, but others told us that additional
training is needed and no amount is ever enough. Although it appears
that additional training options have been made available to local police, the real issues are whether the "right" training is made available
and whether agencies can and do take advantage of it. As one respondent explained,

> More training has been made available for counterterrorism,
> weapons of mass destruction, explosives, and collection and dis-
> semination of intelligence. Conferences are geared more toward
> terrorism now too. However, most analysis is really "case sup-

port." Historically, analysts only provided software-driven link analysis (e.g., who called who). There is no training available to teach analysts how to engage in critical thinking to derive an inference based on link analysis, unless someone from the Central Intelligence Agency or the Drug Enforcement Agency, for example, are hired for training.[8]

The comments above reflect a persistent concern expressed by respondents: As law enforcement officers, they are generally well trained in evidence gathering to support investigation of crimes and, ultimately, prosecution of offenses. They lack training—and even access to training—to help them support the traditional intelligence mission. This training is especially important as agencies become more active regarding gathering information and evidence in ways that may ultimately support traditional intelligence activities.

Another respondent noted the lack of standardization in analytical training across local, state, and federal agencies. These sentiments underscore the general claim that the real weakness in training has to do with analysis. Analysis, as one respondent explained, brings information to the point of understanding and is extremely important and most valuable. Much traditional criminal intelligence is very tactical—tips to connections or locations of suspects. In contrast, the counterterrorism mission requires much more analysis—assessing the validity of information, assembling pieces from various sources to produce a quilt of understanding, then noticing patterns or anomalies that may provide warning.

Moreover, although training options may have become more available, those options are not fully utilized by local police agencies. Some agencies are confident that the training their intelligence personnel receive is already sufficient. Others conduct additional training only when outside funding is available. Thus, the ability to take advantage of training may be limited by the difficulty of identifying and securing grants for training. A third explanation is that the training offered is not what local police truly need. As evident from the cases,

---

[8] Interview with a counterterrorism intelligence source, March 11, 2004.

the main need produced by the counterterrorism mission is instruction in intelligence analysis. Those tasked with counterterrorism responsibilities seek practical training from expert analysts. Several respondents suggested the creation of formal intelligence analysis programs similar to forensic science programs now being conducted in colleges and universities.

Information Sources

A critical element of the counterterrorism function is information. Here, we sought explicitly to deepen the survey results by asking about the usefulness of various sources. Specifically, we asked about the utility of beat and undercover officers; electronic wiretaps; other local, state, and federal agencies; task forces; informants; suspects making a deal; private organizations; citizens; internet searches; FBI weekly intelligence bulletins; and the National Law Enforcement Intelligence System. In general, local police agencies use all these sources and more, but respondents provided specific insights regarding each source.

Beat officers are considered by intelligence officers to be a very good source of information. Some officers are more helpful than others, and all view their assistance as a "two-way street." Beat officers will offer information to intelligence officers, but the intelligence officers must reciprocate. Those who interact and work with citizens are thought to offer particularly good intelligence. Beat officers often do not know that the information they possess is useful, so intelligence officers need to find ways to solicit it from them. Although agencies find undercover officers helpful, the extent ranged widely—from less helpful than beat officers to invaluable.

Respondents' impressions about the utility of electronic wiretaps also varied considerably. Some departments reported not using wiretaps for intelligence gathering purposes or leaving them to the FBI. Others characterized wiretaps as extremely helpful, particularly for cases that were not well developed and that benefited from the information obtained in wiretaps.

The survey results illustrated that the majority of local law enforcement agencies have relied on other local, state, and federal agencies as information sources at least once, and most of those that used these other sources rated them as "somewhat useful." The case study respondents echoed this sentiment. They described other local, state, and federal agencies as good sources of information, but said that they all could be improved. Although there is reliance on and communication among these agencies, at least one respondent felt that each agency does only what it needs to do, which can inhibit the communication process. Task forces are considered a very good source, especially in regard to identifying trends. Each case study police organization is represented on numerous task forces. The survey suggests that these do not always include a JTTF or ATTF. Only 42 percent of local law enforcement agencies surveyed liaise with or are a member of any task force. Of these, 35 percent and 44 percent liaise with or are members of JTTFs and ATTFs, respectively.

Informants provide good information, but the difficulty is finding informants with knowledge pertaining to terrorism. Once identified, they have provided helpful information. Local police have not had a lot of success in obtaining information from suspects willing to provide information regarding terrorism in return for the prospect of lighter treatment for a crime they are facing. This is an area, however, where one respondent thought improvement should be made.

Private organizations also have proved to be a good source of information for local police. Private security officers, reservation and store clerks, and baggage handlers are good examples of private sources with helpful information; they are much more likely than an officer to see or sense something suspicious. Some agencies are trying to develop such relationships by creating seminars to teach businesses about the kinds of information that is most helpful. These seminars have the twofold objective of easing the anxiety of participants while enhancing the likelihood that they will call the police with information. Similarly, local police agencies are working with targeted citizen groups.

Internet searches are an important source of information for local police, and they are conducted frequently (62 percent of the local law enforcement agencies surveyed reported using the internet as an information source). The utility of the FBI weekly intelligence bulletin is less certain.[9] It is used frequently but is considered less useful by some. One respondent indicated that the information is less helpful when it is not specific to a region,[10] and another that it is useful but mostly repetitive.

"Open" sources of information are used extensively by local police organizations. As one respondent explained,

> About 70–80 percent of our intelligence comes from open sources—those open to the public—such as the newspaper, media, internet, public, and community. The media spends billions of dollars on information gathering. The remaining 20–30 percent comes from undercover surveillance, informants, and federal databases (which are developed from operations). Reasonable suspicion must still exist to review open sources—we can't just review them willy-nilly. CNN is a good source because the information is often correct, unlike other stories. All information must be verified. The internet is a source that was not previously used until about five years ago.[11]

Still other sources that local police are utilizing include various multijurisdictional databases, information networks, security and in-

---

[9] These weekly bulletins share sensitive, unclassified information with state and local law enforcement agencies to raise general awareness about terrorism issues. The bulletins are one of nine primary ways in which the FBI shares intelligence and other information with outside agencies. The other eight mechanisms are the Director's Briefing, Intelligence Information Reports, Intelligence Assessments, Secure Video Teleconference System, Urgent Reports, Quarterly Terrorist Threat Assessments, email messages, and Terrorist Watch List. For a description of these sources, see Office of the Inspector General (2003).

[10] A respondent explained that the weekly FBI intelligence bulletins come from the FBI headquarters, and these may or may not contain local information. The local field group of the FBI does not disseminate intelligence bulletins on a regular basis, but when it does it also may or may not contain local information. The content of the bulletins, according to this source, depends on the content of the intelligence. It is not necessarily about the local situation.

[11] Interview with a counterterrorism intelligence source, March 2, 2004.

telligence bulletins and briefings from various agencies (some including other local police departments), think tanks, and intelligence centers. In general, most sources are used every day, and their usefulness depends on the particular case. Some nontraditional sources, such as the internet and baggage handlers, are now used more than in the past. Some sources, such as JTTF databases, are now made available to local police—which was not the case, at least for some departments, before the 9/11 attacks. The acquisition of security clearances by local police has enhanced access to such databases.

Despite the proliferation of information sources, departments remain cautious in collecting information. One respondent commented that before the 9/11 attacks, department intelligence personnel mostly just kept newspaper clippings, and even after the attacks they have been fearful of lawsuits over intelligence collection. Other agencies are also concerned about what information to collect and share. Although the Patriot Act made it easier for the FBI and other federal officers to collect information, some cities oppose the act, thereby leaving local intelligence officers in the awkward position of trying to do their jobs without going against their city's position.[12]

Communication Within and Among LEAs

Local police agencies have developed means of communicating counterterrorism information among personnel, but especially between intelligence and line officers. CDP established an intranet to share information within the organization, and everyone receives a daily bulletin. In turn, patrol officers send information back to intelligence. To facilitate the exchange of valuable information, CDP officers are trained on types of activities to look for (for instance, someone videotaping an airport). Patrol officers know generally what types of in-

---

[12] The Patriot Act, officially titled Uniting and Strengthening America by Providing Appropriate Tools Required to Intercept and Obstruct Terrorism Act, P.L. 107-56, 115 Stat. 272 (2001), relaxed the standards for national security (as opposed to criminal) wiretaps, permitted officials to monitor the source and destination of email and internet traffic, and made it easier for officials to get access to individuals' financial, educational, and other records.

formation are needed by intelligence officers, and they receive specific instruction when necessary. The information flows both ways.

Communication between local police and the FBI has improved since the 9/11 attacks. This has primarily occurred through the FBI's JTTFs: All case study agencies reported assigning at least one person to their local JTTF. It should be noted from the survey results, however, that only 36 percent of local law enforcement agencies surveyed liaised with or were a member of a JTTF.[13] Some had been members long before the 9/11 attacks; others joined only afterward. Regardless, most case study agencies now believe they have excellent two-way communication with the FBI—something that many would not have said before 9/11. They work very closely together, brief each other on cases, and know everything the other knows, all without releasing classified information. In at least one jurisdiction, a member of the FBI works out of the local police agency, and vice versa, and this has worked well in that city. Sometimes the collaboration is formal. Occasionally memorandums of understanding are developed for specific cases. As the survey results indicated, the FBI provides guidance to some but not all local agencies on what information to collect, although some respondents indicated the FBI would provide guidance if they needed it.[14] The FBI has made available additional databases and information sources (for instance, those with overseas information), and local police have provided the FBI with criminal histories.

Personalities and relationships are key to the information sharing process. Interagency communication has been enhanced through good personalities and phone calls to personal contacts. One respondent suggested the importance of having the "right" people involved in the communication process when he explained that prior to the 9/11 attacks, information sharing with the FBI was not good. How-

---

[13] Based on the survey findings, reasons local law enforcement agencies report for coordinating with a JTTF include assisting with an investigation (17 percent), sharing intelligence information (64 percent), receiving counterterrorism training (44 percent), and for other purposes (6 percent).

[14] The survey suggested that two-thirds of local law enforcement agencies received guidance from the FBI concerning intelligence collection.

ever, since then the FBI has placed a new supervisor on the JTTF and now shares much more information with the local agency.

However, bureaucracies and security clearances remain challenges to communication. As one respondent said,

> The major challenge to coordinating with the JTTF is different bureaucracies. When someone asks one of our officers how long it would take to get certain information or accomplish a task, he looks at his watch, while someone from a federal agency would respond to the same question by looking at the calendar.[15]

Security clearances are an issue because important JTTF information is often limited to those with a clearance. Cleared officers need to be creative in how they pass along key information both within and among agencies. Several of the jurisdictions reported that they now have more personnel with security clearances, and this has helped the flow of communication.

In addition to the FBI, local police agencies participate and share information with a plethora of other agencies and task forces—a feature that also came through in the surveys. These include local, regional, and state task forces, security and planning committees, advisory councils, and warning groups. Likewise, local police have coordinated investigations with many other organizations, such as the Bureau of Alcohol, Tobacco, and Firearms; the Departments of Customs, Defense, and State; the Secret Service; the Central Intelligence Agency; the Defense Intelligence Agency; the Drug Enforcement Agency; the Immigration and Naturalization Service; Interpol; the British Home Office; various embassies; Israeli, Egyptian, and Canadian police; other local police; fire agencies; and private groups. Local police therefore do not hesitate to communicate information and coordinate their activities with whoever is necessary.

Understandably, each multiagency collaboration faces its own particular roadblocks, deriving from personalities, egos, culture, politics, policies, city regulations, and the likelihood that all participants

---

[15] Interview with a counterterrorism intelligence source, March 11, 2004.

have their own ideas and want credit for them. Moreover, one respondent described information shared at this level as largely abstract and of little use at the street level. The key obstacle, it appears, is that sometimes too many agencies are involved. A respondent recommended that a single source take the lead on all counterterrorism efforts, with acknowledgment by other agencies of the lead agency's authority. This idea is consistent with the recent 9/11 Commission Report recommendations, at the federal level, to unify intelligence and planning through a national counterterrorism center and a national intelligence director (National Commission on Terrorist Attacks Upon the United States, 2004).[16]

Findings from the Case Studies

In combination with the survey results, the case studies provide insights into how local police authorities have—and have not— changed in seeking better intelligence in the war on terrorism:

- In most cases, the mandate of the counterterrorism function is informal and set by the chain of command.
- These police departments rely on federal guidelines in shaping their intelligence function, but the terrorist threat has raised awareness about what should and can be done in gathering, analyzing, retaining, and disseminating intelligence. This has led some departments to adopt or refine their own guidelines.
- Oversight of the development of counterterrorism intelligence is provided internally through the chain of command in these agencies, but some jurisdictions have developed systematic or at least ad hoc oversight by an external body.
- Local police generally have not created separate units for the counterterrorism function. Counterterrorism intelligence gath-

---

[16] The specific recommendations are summarized in the Executive Summary and spelled out in more detail in chapter 23, "How to Do It? A Different Way of Organizing the Government."

ering and analysis tend to occur as part of a larger criminal intelligence unit, but individuals are assigned to counterterrorism as a functional area.

- The terrorist threat has not led to large-scale changes in the organizational structure of most local police departments.

- These agencies have increased their commitment of human resources to counterterrorism efforts, which usually has come at the expense of other policing areas.

- Additional training has been made available to local police, but not for analysis, which is currently the most important training need.

- Counterterrorism intelligence officers in these organizations use many sources of information on a regular basis but have increased their use of nontraditional sources.

- The 9/11 attacks have led to a significant increase in the amount of counterterrorism information shared within and among local police and their federal counterparts. Paradoxically, though, the sheer number of cooperating agencies sometimes inhibits progress in responding to the terrorist threat.

Emerging Issues

The detailed examination of local LEA counterterrorism intelligence activities reveals several issues that must be addressed. Perhaps most important is the issue of how much these operations are costing local LEAs. We have no detailed cost information, but respondents from most of the case study sites reported that their operations involved significant and uncompensated reallocations of resources. The magnitude of this potential budget constraint is unclear. However, to the extent that communities are spending their own resources on counterterrorism intelligence, the model may not be sustainable as the memory and urgency of the September 11 attacks recede and communities struggle with local budget priorities.

There is a second reason that local investment in counterterrorism intelligence may not be sustainable: a potential conflict between LEAs' crime prevention mandate and the demands of homeland security support missions. Since the 9/11 attacks, the demands on LEAs have changed in multiple ways. As described earlier in this chapter, LEAs report spending their own resources on intelligence (and other homeland security) support activities. Such expenditures could in turn affect the ability to prevent and respond to ordinary crime by, for example, reducing the amount that agencies have to spend on patrol or detective functions. There are other ways in which LEAs have been affected by 9/11. For example, some agencies are considering changing policies and procedures to support federal immigration control and deportation efforts.[17] Before 9/11, many departments had explicit policies not to arrest and detain people if their only crime concerned their immigration status. Other agencies are affected by losing key personnel to the Iraq war effort. Still others are finding it difficult to compete against the private and federal sectors for the recruitment of officers.

Unfortunately, there is no analysis on the tradeoff between homeland security and crime prevention activities, so no conclusions can be drawn about the effect that post–9/11 missions are having on crime. Indeed, some of the case study respondents drew conclusions in the opposite direction. They pointed out that their organization was not investing purely in counterterrorism intelligence, but rather in intelligence more broadly. For some departments, the intelligence capability was embedded in a major crimes unit; in others it is embedded in an organized crime unit. Thus, some make the argument

---

[17] The proposed CLEAR Act (Clear Law Enforcement for Criminal Alien Removal) (H.R. 2671) provides incentives for state and local authorities to assist federal authorities with immigration enforcement. The bill encourages local and state police departments to enforce immigration laws against aliens discovered in the course of their normal law enforcement duties. Many departments, such as the Los Angeles Police Department, prohibit such immigration enforcement support. As of March 2005, LAPD was rewriting its guidelines to allow more latitude for immigration enforcement support (see "LAPD Clarifying Rule on Immigrants," *Los Angeles Times,* March 31 2005, available at http://www.indybay.org/news/2005/03/1730575.php, accessed on May 23, 2005). Still other jurisdictions, such as Ann Arbor, Mich., continue to prohibit such support ("Resolution to Protest the Eroding of Civil Liberties Under the USA Patriot Act (Public Law 107-56) and Related Federal Orders Since 9/11/01," approved by the Ann Arbor City Council on July 7, 2003).

that post–9/11 policing missions are actually helping with traditional crime prevention missions by building skills and capabilities relevant to crime prevention.

Ultimately, the tension between maintaining traditional law enforcement missions and expanding or building counterterrorism intelligence support operations must be examined in greater detail. It is important to investigate the processes by which LEAs support and execute their counterterrorism intelligence support functions. It is important to understand how, or if, these intelligence functions can be sustained, and at what and whose cost. We cannot complete such an assessment in this document. We can only point out the importance of conducting it.

Finally, a part of that investigation must be a careful assessment of the authorization and oversight environment and the contributions—however qualitatively measured—that state and local LEA intelligence activities make to disrupting and preventing terrorism. What kinds of cases and operations do LEA intelligence activities contribute to? Chapter Four provides an initial analysis of some of these benefit issues.

Oversight and Its Implications

Oversight of state and local intelligence activities is mostly ad hoc and informal. It is generally conducted through the LEA's chain of command, although some departments have "outside" review bodies, such the LAPD's civilian committee approving undercover operations. The courts have not been active in overseeing state and local activities. That may be in large part because most intelligence gathering—especially that not predicated on a crime having been committed—is done by federal officials, through federal authorizations, which is only sometimes done in cooperation with state and local officials. Thus, this chapter first looks at one particular—and particularly sensitive—form of information gathering, wiretapping, at the local and state level compared with the federal level. In so doing, the chapter suggests an "ideal" pattern of cooperation between the various levels of government in the intelligence aspects of the war on terrorism. It concludes with recommendations about what would be needed to approach that ideal.

Patterns of Surveillance and Oversight

The survey and case studies portray a varied set of state and, especially, local responses to the threat of terrorism. For many—perhaps most—of the localities surveyed, terrorism is a threat that has yet to come. Overall, however, state and local intelligence gathering has increased, at least as measured by wiretaps or other communications interceptions for law enforcement purposes. Not surprisingly, as Table 4.1 indicates, the jump was sharpest from 2000 to 2001. Since 2001, the number of orders has stayed roughly constant, but the number of communications intercepted under each order has risen sharply, nearly tripling from 2000 to 2003.

Table 4.1 reports the numbers of intercept orders for law enforcement purposes approved by federal, state, and local judges, respectively, along with the average number of communications intercepted per order. The sixth column of the table reports the number of federal intercept orders granted for national security purposes under the Foreign Intelligence Surveillance Act, or FISA. Modern presidents have claimed the need for warrantless searches for national security purposes as opposed to law enforcement, but the courts called them into question. Enacted in 1978, FISA was a compromise, establishing a special secret court to review applications for national security search and wiretaps of both citizens and noncitizens. The Patriot Act of 2001 widened the scope for FISA warrants.

There has been considerable attention to privacy and civil liberties considerations at the federal level, especially after the Patriot Act,

Table 4.1
Federal, State, and Local Wiretap Orders, 2000–2003

Year	Federal Orders		State and Local Orders		FISA Orders
	No.	Communications Intercepted per Order (average)	No.	Communications Intercepted per Order (average)	No.
2000	479	NA	711	NA	1,005
2001	486	2,367	1,005	1,180	932
2002	497	2,354	861	1,335	1,228
2003	578	2,931	864	3,052	1,724

SOURCES: Administrative Office of the U.S. Courts, Wiretap Reports, available at http://www.uscourts.gov/library/wiretap.html, accessed June 14, 2004; for FISA, see http://www.fas.org/irp/agency/doj/fisa/index.html#rept, accessed June 14, 2004. The 2003 report on FISA surveillance from the Justice Department to the Administrative Office of the U.S. Courts is available at http://www.fas.org/irp/agency/doj/fisa/2003rept.pdf, accessed June 14, 2004.

which widened authority not just for FISA but also for investigation and surveillance in other ways. Indeed, the FISA court itself made the first appeal ever under the FISA act. The court was concerned that the Patriot Act had eliminated the "wall" between law enforcement and intelligence or national security at the FBI and Justice Department. The review court rejected the appeal and let officials working on law enforcement and FISA surveillance continue to share information.[1] In contrast, there has been much less attention to what is going on, or what might be authorized, at the state and local level, and virtually no research on law and practice at those levels.[2]

The numbers in Table 4.1 should be read with some caution. First, the state and local numbers probably understate the facts, for several reasons. In 2001, for instance, 46 states had laws permitting interceptions, but only 25 reported using that authority. And if the states underreport to the federal government, so, too, localities may underreport to the states. Second, the purpose of the interceptions is not evident because terrorism is a problem for both intelligence and law enforcement. Thus, while by definition the FISA taps were for intelligence rather than law enforcement purposes, they may have generated leads or other information relevant to criminal prosecution. More to the point, while many states are in the process of broadening their authority to intercept communications, in most places the purpose is usually law enforcement. If the wiretaps generate information that is useful in the war on terrorism but not germane to any ongoing criminal investigation, that information is a by-product.

From our interviews with local police departments—Las Vegas, for instance—it seemed likely that if local officials undertook terrorism-related surveillance for intelligence purposes, they almost always did so with federal officials through the JTTFs. If so, the request for surveillance presumably would go through FISA channels, and any subsequent oversight would be through the federal courts.

---

[1] See *In Re: Sealed Case No. 02-001, 02-002*, Federal Intelligence Surveillance Court of Review, 2002, 310 F.3d 717.

[2] One exception is Kennedy and Swire (2003). This article, too, notes the lack of research on the topic.

The role of state courts in overseeing police investigations usually comes in the form of Fourth Amendment litigation arising from a criminal prosecution. It has been—and probably will continue to be—rare to see state courts ruling on the constitutionality of post–9/11 legislation like the Patriot Act.

In fact, a search turned up only one case of a state court ruling related to a post–9/11 issue. In that case, civil liberties groups sued New Jersey counties that held detainees for the (then) Immigration and Naturalization Service (INS) in county jails, seeking disclosure of information on detainees pursuant to state disclosure laws. The New Jersey court rejected the suit, largely on the grounds that federal authority preempted state action.[3] If surveillance is done through FISA, however, federal officials are responsible, and state courts will rarely have an opportunity to rule on the conduct of those federal officials. It can happen: Federal officers acting pursuant to federal legislation could obtain evidence that a state later uses in a criminal prosecution. A state court could rule on the constitutionality of the federal officers' conduct (and thus on the federal legislation itself). But this would be rare.

Expanding Surveillance

The recent sharp increase in surveillance at the state and local levels may represent mostly enhanced law enforcement, with terrorism as one motivation among several. But many states are expanding their interception authorities, again for many purposes. Thus, the range of issues associated with this form of intelligence gathering will only grow—all the more so because, as the Patriot Act and other measures widen the scope for surveillance at the federal level, states are almost bound to expand their own authorities.

Especially at the state and local levels, laws address three kinds of surveillance techniques. The first is bugging (placing a listening de-

---

[3] See 352 N.J. Super.44, 799 A.2d 629.

vice near a target conversation) or wiretapping (intercepting the conversation during its transmission). Both are subject to a Fourth Amendment test: Is there a "reasonable expectation of privacy standard" so as to make the interception a "search" under the amendment? The second is monitoring the recipient ("pen register") or originator ("trap and trace") of a message without reading its contents. The Supreme Court held in 1979 that this monitoring was not subject to a "reasonable expectation of privacy" and thus is not subject to the probable cause standard for searches under the Fourth Amendment. So, too, the Fourth Amendment has not been interpreted to prevent third parties—banks, telephone companies, or internet service providers—from voluntarily turning over to law enforcement agencies stored records in their hands.

Since the 1960s, federal legislation and federal courts have set standards for state and local eavesdropping. The two central measures are (1) the Berger decision by the Supreme Court in 1967, which established the Fourth Amendment standard that the eavesdropping must be justified on the basis of "probable cause" that a crime had been or was about to be committed, and (2) the Electronic Communications Privacy Act of 1986 (ECPA), which updated the standards for newer technologies, such as cell phones and email.[4] States were supposed to enact standards that closely track these federal requirements, but it was not clear—even before 9/11—that state law and practice routinely did contain the protections of federal standards and procedures.

After 9/11, many states began to discuss more permissive reforms of their wiretap legislation.[5] Those measures typically expanded what crimes would justify wiretaps; who could grant authority; who could implement taps; and authorization to conduct "roving" taps

---

[4] *Berger v. New York*, 388 U.S. 42, 54–55. 58–59 (1967); and Electronic Communication Privacy Act of 1986, P.L. 99-508, 100 Stat. 1848 (1986).

[5] The Web site of the Constitution Project Initiative on Liberty and Security provides information on the status of each state's wiretap legislation, along with an overview across states. See http://www.ncsl.org/programs/lis/CIP/surveillance.htm, accessed September 8, 2005.

across broader geographic areas, as well as the devices subject to interception.

The last measure, expanding authority to new devices, merely brings state laws into line with ECPA; the issues raised mostly concern whether local officials will get the training needed to operate such taps. Similarly, "roving" taps that permit surveillance of any communications device the target may use, instead of specifying a particular telephone or the like, are mostly a modernization of legislation. Roving taps were permitted under ECPA but not under FISA until the Patriot Act brought the two into harmony. States are now moving to modernize their statutes in the same way. This does imply, though, that just as federal judges can issue orders for the entire nation, some states are permitting judges to issue orders that extend beyond the jurisdictional bounds of their courts. Florida, Virginia, and Maryland have such provisions.[6] Although these provisions recognize the fact that terrorism respects few boundaries, they do raise the prospects of "judge shopping" and of lessened supervision of interceptions performed beyond the originating court's jurisdiction.

Most of the state amendments and proposed amendments add computer crimes, terrorism, and various terrorism-related crimes to the list of offenses for which interception may be sought. This expansion is consistent with ECPA, which lists a number of crimes but includes other crimes not specifically mentioned that are punishable by imprisonment for more than one year. It raises a concern parallel to the one at the federal level—that terrorism is hard to define and thus often defined loosely—amplified by concern that state and local procedures lack federal safeguards.

ECPA permits states to grant the right to seek interception orders down to "the principal prosecuting attorney of any political subdivision," and state statutes already vary widely in how centralized that granting is. Some states permit county prosecutors to request interceptions, and most of the initiatives under consideration would increase, rather than constrain, the dispersal of authority. A New

---

[6] Kennedy and Swire (2003), p. 982.

York proposal, for instance, would grant request authority to the chief counsel of temporary state investigating commissions.[7]

Who implements the tap—often called the *monitor*—is also critical in keeping logs on the tap and shutting it off when conversation becomes privileged or is not related to the crime. ECPA limits monitors to officers having responsibility for investigating the offense in question but does permit the use of contractors as monitors provided they are under the supervision of such officers. Most of the post–9/11 state proposals have sought to expand the use of contractors or retired law enforcement officers.

Funds in several categories of the Department of Homeland Security's Office of Domestic Preparedness (ODP) budget include grant expenditures for intelligence and related items, such as surveillance equipment. The fiscal year 2004 ODP Terrorism Prevention Program ($500 million) is available to all states and localities; the 2004 Urban Areas High Security Initiative ($750 million) has another set of guidelines. State and local LEAs will be looking to grant programs such as these to enhance their capabilities, so the guidelines will encourage many questions based on what capabilities the agencies expect to develop and how those new or expanded activities will be overseen.

Approaching an Ideal in Intelligence Relations Among Levels of Government

What does all this flux in procedures amount to? One way to evaluate that question is to pose an ideal pattern or division of labor among the levels of government and to use it to evaluate what is actually going on. That evaluation, in turn, suggests steps that might be taken to move closer to the ideal.

---

[7] Kennedy and Swire (2003), p. 979.

Mandate and Oversight

Given FISA, federal authorities—the FBI in particular—will naturally lead in intelligence gathering that is not connected to criminal investigation. Local officials have neither money nor capacity for that kind of pure or traditional intelligence. So, too, that kind of intelligence gathering would be guided by federal regulations ad overseen primarily by federal courts. Here, the current pattern is close to the ideal.

Ideally, state and local authorities would conduct two kinds of information or intelligence gathering—investigation of possible criminal acts, including electronic surveillance; and collection that is incident to the normal activities of LEA officers. The latter comes through the eyes and ears of the cops on the beat, and the goal is domain awareness—what is going on in their jurisdiction, what the state of possible targets is, and so on. Here, there are several deviations from the ideal. Perhaps most important, the line between intelligence and law enforcement remains blurred for state and local agencies, particularly because law enforcement agencies seek to prevent terrorist crimes, not enforce the laws against them after the fact. Compounding the problem is the enormous range of state reporting on eavesdropping—let alone state regulation. Finally, the guidelines depart from the ideal in significant ways. We saw from the case studies that most of the guidelines for the counterterrorism mission at the local level are ad hoc and derive from the local chain of command. This implies that there is relatively little federal oversight over a dynamic, but important, regulatory process.

Sharing Information

The more practical shortfall is that local LEAs get neither much guidance about what to look for nor enough intelligence that is specific enough to shape local operations. There has been considerable attention given to sharing information, especially looking from the federal level down, for instance by the national 9/11 Commission. It reflects the by now common wisdom that the problem is only apparently one of information exchange, and the processes to support it. To be sure, effective information exchange remains a considerable problem, especially for many local departments, which have difficulty enough communicating with one another. But policy and guidelines are the more formidable obstacles. The 9/11 Commission recommended creating a government-wide "trusted information network" to share information horizontally, on the model suggested by the Markle Foundation Task Force (2003). Yet, as both the surveys and cases suggested, the principal information-sharing mechanism, the JTTF, is constrained because it requires getting the state and local participants security clearances at the level of their FBI counterparts. It is imperative to find new ways to share information and to share it more widely. The 9/11 Commission notes that intelligence analysts, like other professionals, want to play at the top of their games, so their reports inevitably begin with the most classified—and thus least sharable—information. The commission suggests the opposite, starting any report by separating information from sources and writing first at the level that can be most easily shared. If intelligence consumers wanted more, they could query the system under whatever rules were in place, leaving an audit trail of requests. At present, many, perhaps most, potential consumers would not even know what to ask for.

Analyzing Information

Secretary of Defense Donald Rumsfeld has focused attention in the intelligence war on terrorism to the "known unknowns," the things we know we don't know, and, especially to the "unknown unknowns," the things we don't know we don't know. Yet much of the 9/11 failure turned on another category, the "unknown knowns," the things we didn't know or had forgotten we knew. One of the striking findings from the surveys and cases is the importance of more analysis across all of Rumsfeld's categories.

That importance derives directly from the nature of the counterterrorism task. A traditional law enforcement investigation seeks to reconstruct the single trail from crime back to perpetrator. In contrast, the counterterrorism task, especially prevention, needs to look at a number of paths, assembling enough information about each to know when patterns are changing or something suspicious is afoot along one of the paths. It is not only an intelligence-rich task. It is also a task rich in intelligence analysis.

Ideally, the analysis function would be split among the levels of government. The federal level has a comparative advantage in special sources, especially sources abroad. Its analysis will naturally concentrate on those and on the broad, "connect the dots" function. Sometimes, those sources and that analysis will provide warning specific enough to alert particular local authorities. In other cases, though, it will remain general and will serve mostly to tip off local officials about what they might look for—for example, a string of apparently unrelated crimes involving false identities.

The federal government is struggling, through the National Counterterrorism Center and DHS as well as a greatly expanded FBI intelligence function, to do better at its part of the ideal. But it is striking how limited the analytic capacity is at the local level. Only the very largest police departments have any at all. Yet, the ideal local role in the division of analytic labor would be to take the general guidance provided by federal officials and relate it to local domain awareness.

CHAPTER FIVE

Policy Implications

Our survey revealed that counterterrorism intelligence activity, and the response to homeland security demands more generally, is concentrated in larger departments. The case studies provided details on how LEAs organize, manage, and resource these activities. LEAs are not generally engaged in substantive reorganizations around the issue of counterterrorism intelligence but are typically reallocating resources from other demands and functions. They generally report that they are not receiving explicit federal support and are paying for the activity out of internal reallocations. Finally, the chapter on oversight and its implications revealed that there has been a substantial increase in state and local involvement in wiretap activity and that the federal courts almost always retain oversight authority.

The picture of law enforcement involvement in counterterrorism intelligence is somewhat mixed. On the one hand, relatively few LEAs appear to be supporting intelligence activities to any great extent. This suggests that the "problem" of police intelligence is not as pervasive as some fear. On the other hand, there has been a marked increase in intelligence activity among those departments that are engaged in it. In addition, with the activity concentrated in the largest departments, a substantial portion of the American population may be in jurisdictions with active intelligence programs.

The findings and countervailing tensions noted above suggest four major issues concerning LEA intelligence activity that need to be addressed: resourcing, training, development of doctrine, and guidance from the courts concerning civil liberties.

Resourcing

It is not clear that the current model of funding LEA counterterrorism intelligence (and, more generally, LEA homeland security missions) is sustainable. On the one hand, municipalities consistently report that they are redirecting traditional crime-control resources to support homeland security missions. These redirections have unknown consequences for staffing, morale, and preparedness for traditional missions of crime prevention and response. On the other hand, some LEAs report the possibility that counterterrorism intelligence activities may hold the promise of increasing the agency's effectiveness against organized crime, drug trafficking, and gang activity by building skills that are critical to confronting such problems.

To our knowledge, no credible analysis of the consequences of increased counterterrorism intelligence activity (and homeland security activity more generally) for routine law enforcement missions has been performed. Similarly, we did not find any analyses that addressed the extent to which local agencies are diverting funding from traditional activities to intelligence and homeland security support. Evidence in these areas remains anecdotal. These deficiencies should be remedied so that we may begin to determine the costs and benefits of current methods of funding LEA counterterrorism intelligence activities.

Training

The obvious first need is more training for expanded intelligence capacity, especially in analysis, at the state and local level. Training would include techniques for increasing domain awareness and for undertaking local threat assessments. So far, however, federal assistance programs have tended to emphasize equipment for consequence management, not training for intelligence, although that state of affairs is changing. Training would also address the other visible concern—the varied and ad hoc nature of guidelines for counter-terrorism intelligence.

Here the *National Criminal Intelligence Sharing Plan* guidelines (BJA, 2003) are especially relevant and provide a reminder that the training must occur at both the individual and organizational levels. Key recommendations include:

- Each LEA should have a clearly articulated mission statement with respect to counterterrorism intelligence.
- LEAs should adopt 28 CFR Part 23 (Criminal Intelligence Systems Operating Policies) as the *minimum* standard for their data collection efforts.
- LEAs should adopt Law Enforcement Intelligence Unit, Criminal Intelligence File Guidelines as the model for file maintenance.
- All LEA intelligence personnel should be trained to the standards contained in the *National Criminal Intelligence Sharing Plan*.

Finally, it is worth noting that *centralized* training might permit improved oversight. As discussed in earlier chapters, oversight mechanisms are largely a product of local decisionmaking processes and are typically tailored to the specific community. A central training program would permit improved cross-jurisdiction comparisons and give federal authorities greater insight into the myriad formulations of local intelligence programs.

Developing Doctrine

Currently, the process of developing, organizing, and managing state and local participation in counterterrorism intelligence is ad hoc. Most localities develop their own policies and procedures without strong guidance on many issues. It seems likely that there will be an increasing need for doctrine, or fundamental principles, to guide federal, state, and local actions in support of counterterrorism intelligence.

Since most LEAs participate in counterterrorism intelligence processes through the JTTFs, the task forces are one logical mechanism for developing doctrine. There are other ways that the federal government can encourage the development of doctrine. For example, greater and more explicit federal funding for state and local intelligence agencies would permit a greater regulatory role over what is now a fairly loose and ad hoc process. Such a structure would encourage local police to develop internal guidelines and external oversight by tying them to funding.

Similarly, although law enforcement throughout the United States is fundamentally local in structure, there is no reason that law enforcement intelligence needs to be. A federal intelligence support program could operate with the federal government paying the cost of an "intelligence supervisor" for eligible law enforcement agencies. Such a supervisor would have a role analogous to that of the federal security director at airports. The federal representative provides day-to-day operational security direction of the airport, even though general airport operations are typically a local function. The intelligence supervisor could be selected by national authorities (such as the FBI) and trained to national intelligence standards.

These three models for defining a federal role (using JTTFs, linking funding to standards, developing a national intelligence program) are not an exhaustive list of options. Nor should their mention here be construed as endorsing any particular approach.[1] Indeed, none of them addresses the role that DHS and other agencies should have in interacting with LEAs. Nevertheless, these models represent an important reminder of the need to clarify the federal role in the state and local counterterrorism intelligence process.

---

[1] Geller and Morris (1992) report on some of the pitfalls of federal regulatory efforts with state and local LEAs. See also Reiss (1992).

Civil Liberties and Guidance from the Courts

Finally, we acknowledge that this document has paid scant attention to critical issues of civil liberties and the role of the courts in shaping state and local counterterrorism intelligence functions. On the former, it seemed important to document what law enforcement agencies were doing on the intelligence front before we engaged in an analysis of the effect on civil liberties. Thus, we leave the complex issue of the intersection of state and local intelligence and fundamental liberties to subsequent researchers.

More generally, these issues will increasingly be decided by the courts, and it will be up to them—the federal courts in particular—to continue assessing whether the relaxed procedures of the intelligence war on terrorism are striking the correct balance between privacy and civil liberties, on the one hand, and security on the other. Our survey and case studies hint at what becomes much more explicit in conversation with federal homeland security intelligence officials. They feel they have little guidance when deciding what they should do with information they collect—especially about American citizens. Can they keep it in databases, and for how long and on what basis? It will be up to the courts to enforce guidelines when constitutional or statutory standards apply, and to put pressure on the executive branch to issue clear guidelines when such standards do not apply.

References

The Advisory Panel to Assess Domestic Response Capabilities for Terrorism Involving Weapons of Mass Destruction ("Gilmore Commission"), Reports 1–5, 1999–2004. Available at http://www.rand.org/nsrd/terrpanel/, accessed September 5, 2005.

Berkowitz, Bruce D., and Allen E. Goodman. *Best Truths: Intelligence in the Information Age.* New Haven, Conn.: Yale University Press, 2000.

Bureau of Justice Assistance (BJA). *National Criminal Intelligence Sharing Plan, Executive Summary.* Washington, D.C.: U.S. Department of Justice Office of Justice Programs, 2003. Available at http://it.ojp.gov/topic.jsp?topic_id=103, accessed September 8, 2005.

Bureau of Justice Statistics (BJS). *Census of State and Local Law Enforcement Agencies, 2000.* Washington, D.C.: U.S. Department of Justice Bureau of Justice Statistics Bulletin NCJ 194066, 2002.

Chalk, Peter, and William Rosenau. *Confronting "The Enemy Within": Security Intelligence, the Police, and Counterterrorism in Four Democracies.* Santa Monica, Calif.: RAND Corporation, MG-100-RC, 2004.

Davis, Lois M., K. Jack Riley, Gregory Kirk Ridgeway, Jennifer E. Pace, Sarah K. Cotton, Paul S. Steinberg, Kelly Damphousse, and Brent L. Smith. *When Terrorism Hits Home: How Prepared Are State and Local Law Enforcement?* Santa Monica, Calif.: RAND Corporation, MG-104-MIPT, 2004.

Davis, Lois M., Lou T. Mariano, Jennifer Pace, Sarah K. Cotton, and Paul Steinberg. "Summary of Selected Survey Results." Appendix D in The Advisory Panel to Assess Domestic Response Capabilities for Terrorism Involving Weapons of Mass Destruction, Fifth Annual Report to the

President and Congress, *V. Forging America's New Normalcy: Securing Our Homeland, Protecting Our Liberty*. Arlington, Va.: RAND Corporation, 2003.

Department of Homeland Security (DHS). Press Release: "Secretary Ridge Addresses National Governors Association." Washington, D.C.: Office of the Press Secretary, DHS, August 18, 2003.

Executive Order on Critical Infrastructure Protection. Washington, D.C.: The White House, October 16, 2001.

Geller William A., and Norval Morris. "Relations Between Federal and Local Police." In Michael Tonry and Norval Morris (eds.), *Modern Policing, Crime and Justice: A Review of Research*, Vol. 15. Chicago: University of Chicago Press, 1992, pp. 231–348.

Glenn, Russell W., Barbara R. Panitch, Dionne Barnes-Proby, Elizabeth F. Williams, John Christian, Matthew W. Lewis, Scott Gerwehr, and David Brannan. *Training the 21st Century Police Officer: Redefining Police Professionalism for the Los Angeles Police Department*. Santa Monica, Calif.: RAND Corporation, MR-1745-LAPD, 2003.

Global Justice Information Sharing Initiative. *Law Enforcement Analytic Standards*. Richmond, Va.: Global Justice Information Sharing Initiative and International Association of Law Enforcement Intelligence Analysts, Inc., November 2004.

Government Accountability Office (GAO). *Homeland Security: Efforts to Increase Information Sharing Need to Be Strengthened*. Report to the Secretary of Homeland Security. Washington, D.C.: GAO-03-760, 2003.

Hollywood, John S., Diane Snyder, Kenneth McKay, and John E. Boon. *Out of the Ordinary: Finding Hidden Threats by Analyzing Unusual Behavior*. Santa Monica, Calif.: RAND Corporation, MG-126-RC, 2004.

Joint Task Force on Intelligence and Law Enforcement. *Report to the Attorney General and Director of Central Intelligence* ("Rindskopf-Richards Report"). May 1995. Available at http://www.cnss.org/Rindskopf-Richards%20report.pdf, accessed September 13, 2005.

Kennedy, Charles H., and Peter P. Swire. "State Wiretaps and Electronic Surveillance After September 11." *Hastings Law Journal*, Vol. 54, 2003, pp. 971–985.

Libicki, Martin C., and Shari Lawrence Pfleeger. *Collecting the Dots: Problem Formulation and Solution Elements.* Santa Monica, Calif.: RAND Corporation, OP-103-RC, 2004.

Markle Foundation Task Force. *Creating a Trusted Network for Homeland Security.* New York: Markle Foundation, December 2003.

Martin, Kate. "Justice Department Fails to Address 9/11 Intelligence Failures." Washington, D.C.: Center for National Security Studies, April 2004.

Mueller, Robert S., III, Director, Federal Bureau of Investigation. "Testimony Before the United States Senate Committee on the Judiciary, Sunset Provisions of the USA Patriot Act," April 5, 2005. Available at http://www.fbi.gov/congress/congress05/mueller040505.htm, accessed May 23, 2005.

National Commission on Terrorism. *Countering the Changing Threat of International Terrorism.* Washington, D.C., 2000. Available at http://www.fas.org/irp/threat/commission.html, accessed September 22, 2005.

National Commission on Terrorist Attacks Upon the United States. *The 9/11 Commission Report.* Washington, D.C., 2004. Available at http://www.9-11commission.gov/, accessed August 2, 2004.

Office of the Inspector General, U.S. Department of Justice. *The Federal Bureau of Investigation's Efforts to Improve the Sharing of Intelligence and Other Information.* Washington, D.C.: Office of the Inspector General, December 2003.

Personick, Stewart D., and Cynthia A. Patterson, eds. *Critical Information Infrastructure Protection and the Law: An Overview of Key Issues.* Washington, D.C.: National Academies Press, 2003.

Reiss, Albert J. "Police Organization in the Twentieth Century." In Michael Tonry and Norval Morris (eds.), *Modern Policing, Crime and Justice: A Review of Research*, Vol. 15. Chicago: University of Chicago Press, 1992, pp. 51–90.

Riley, K. Jack, and Bruce Hoffman. *Domestic Terrorism: A National Assessment of State and Local Law Enforcement Preparedness.* Santa Monica, Calif.: RAND Corporation, MR-505-NIJ, 1995.

Treverton, Gregory F. *Reshaping National Intelligence for an Age of Information.* Cambridge, UK: Cambridge University Press, 2003.

Shelby, Senator Richard C. "September 11 and the Imperative of Reform in the U.S. Intelligence Community: Additional Views of Senator Richard C. Shelby, Vice Chairman, Senate Select Committee on Intelligence." In U.S. Senate Select Committee on Intelligence and U.S. Permanent Select Committee on Intelligence, Congressional Reports: Joint Inquiry into Intelligence Community Activities Before and After the Terrorist Attacks of September 11, 2001, December 2002. Available at www.gpoaccess. gov/serialset/creports/911.html, accessed September 5, 2005.

Wildhorn, Sorrel, Brian Michael Jenkins, and Marvin Lavin. *Intelligence Constraints of the 1970s and Domestic Terrorism*. Vol. I, *Effects on the Incidence, Investigation, and Prosecution of Terrorist Activity*. Santa Monica, Calif.: RAND Corporation, N-1901-DOJ, 1982.